CASS LIBRARY OF AFRICAN STUDIES

GENERAL STUDIES

No. 33

Editorial Adviser : JOHN RALPH WILLIS

Omone, son of Chief Benebo of Buguma, in the costume of
the Peri play

SOME NIGERIAN FERTILITY CULTS

P. AMAURY TALBOT

FRANK CASS & CO. LTD.
1967

ed by

OMPANY LIMITED
eet, London WC1
'ord University Press.

First edition   1927
New impression   1967

Printed in Holland by
N. V. Grafische Industrie Haarlem

PREFACE

THE facts collected here are almost exclusively such as came to my notice in the course of the ordinary administrative work in Degama Division, to which I was posted in June, 1914.

The region is mainly inhabited by sections of the two great tribes of Ibo and Ijaw. A full description of these will be given later, but it appeared best to issue without further delay this little monograph, dealing with a certain aspect of their religion, the publication of which has already been long postponed owing in the first place to the war and then to pressure of other work.

As regards the remaining tribes, the subject will be found discussed in other books, especially the *Ethnological Sketch*, comprising the second and third volumes of *The Peoples of Southern Nigeria*, published by the Clarendon Press. The descriptive parts in the following pages were written by my first wife.

P. A. T.

June, 1925.

CONTENTS

LIST OF ILLUSTRATIONS

I

THE GREAT DRUM

THE outbreak of war seemed a favourable opportunity for discontented natives to throw off the restraints imposed by Government and return to old customs, and disturbances occurred in various parts of Nigeria. One of these took place in Aba District to the north-east of Degama. We have since learned that the native name for this region is Aba-Ala, *i.e.* Aba of the Earth Goddess Ale or Ala. Here two messengers employed by the Native Courts were seized and dragged before the great drum, described as from 18 to 20 feet in length, which stood in one of the Juju houses. Later, reliable testimony declared this to have been one of the principal shrines of the Earth Mother herself.

According to the account given us, the unfortunate victims were forced to kneel at the end of the long, trough-like base, from the centre of which the rounded portion of the drum was carved, and their heads struck off so that they fell forward into the cavity. The drum was then splashed with blood and the heads, still bearing the uniform caps, were placed thereon amid the skulls of former victims as a defiance to British rule, which, the insurgents hoped, was no longer powerful enough to protect its servants.

Shortly afterwards, a policeman passing through the region with a prisoner, whom he was bringing down to Degama, was also seized and done to death. Vengeance, swift and sure, followed these crimes. By order of the Resident, the blood-stained drum was burnt to ashes and justice meted out to the guilty persons. The destruction of this fetish was an act of necessity, since no other measures would have produced the same effect upon its worshippers; yet the step was taken with great regret, for the drum was of an interesting type and most elaborately carved.

Some weeks later our road led us through the town of Ihie, where we came upon a similar drum, of a kind then new to us. Cleft from an even larger trunk than the Ibibio big drum at Jamestown, to which it showed some points of resemblance, the giant bole extended at both ends in a Noah's Ark-like base, on which were seated, at either extremity, a male and female figure—the latter holding a babe in her extended arms. (See Fig. 1.)

We were informed that the name of the drum, and of the cult, was Ikoro (or Ikuru). One of the chief towns devoted to its worship was Ohambele nearby. ' This town,' in the words of Mr. B. M. Pepple,

has a big Ikoro drum which is highly respected. Before Government came, they gave it human sacrifices, but now only goats and fowls. They beat this drum during war time. Any human head cut off in war is brought and placed on the drum with blood. No man can see the big Ikoro drum unless he has cut off a human head and presented it to this. It does not matter whether the head was got by war or not. The Ikoro play falls twice a year. The first is called Mkpukpu-Chi (thanksgiving) and falls at harvest time. The second is carried out in the farming season, and is called

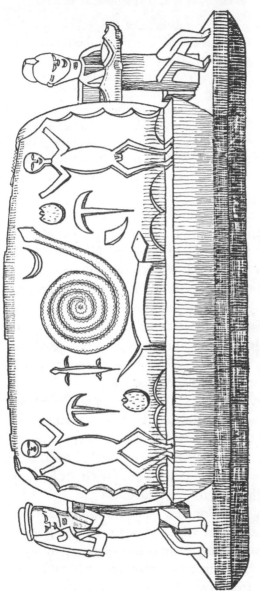

Fig. 1. Ikuru drum at Ihie

Omehie Ogugu (remembrance of the Juju Ogugu). Any man in the town has the right to dance the Ikoro. The big Ikoro is beaten in the house, while the dancers keep outside. Those men, who had cut off a human head, would come to the front of the big Ikoro house and play their motion by raising the sword and telling of the brave deeds they have done; then they would begin to dance again. The Ikoro drum was never carried to another town. Before the time of Government small towns did not make an Ikoro drum. If any small town ventured to do so, the big towns fought them and seized the drum.

Detailed examination of the drum at Ihie showed that the ornamentation carved in relief was of exceptional interest. In the middle, between the figures of a man and woman rudely enough represented and probably depicting the carver and his wife, who were usually sacrificed on the completion of the work, was the carefully chiselled shape of a great serpent folded round on round. On either side of this, various symbols were to be seen, several of which were easily enough recognised as the crescent moon, the sacred crocodile, a Juju horn, and, what seemed to our eager imagination, a fresh example of the double-headed axe, but which was explained by the natives as a musical instrument called, in Ibo, Igilla. The reason why, on closer investigation, our interpretation rather than theirs seemed to be the right one, will be stated later. For the moment our attention was caught by an object quite new to us, the meaning of which we could not even conjecture. On asking its significance we were told simultaneously and with like positiveness from two different sides, one that it was a representation of the familiar tortoise, while the other volunteered the unexpected statement that it pictured the labia majora, with the clitoris showing between.

Those who voiced the opinion first given asked contemptuously whether it was not a matter of common knowledge that tortoise played an important part in the greater number of Jujus. On this, the second party subsided for the moment as if abashed by their opponents, but later one came in private to point out that tortoise is depicted with the crossed lines which indicate the cracks in her shell, whereas in this case the small vertical dashes are the conventional representation of hair. He further explained that the opposition party was right to a certain extent, in that tortoise herself symbolises the feminine generative organs, just as the serpent is well known to typify the phallus.

Till then, the presence of the impaled tortoise before most Jujus, even remotely concerned with the granting of fertility, had been more or less of a puzzle; for, although the snake is recognised by anthropologists as the phallic emblem, no widespread feminine symbol of like significance appears to have been known here hitherto.

The supremacy of tortoise in most tales of African origin has often proved puzzling to folklorists. The subject is mentioned in *The Times Literary Supplement* of 10th December, 1914:

There is one very curious point which these and other stories of the kind have in common—that though these professional jokers, so to call them, have the better of all

the animals with whom they ordinarily enter into a contest
of wits, there is one . . . who always has the better of them
all, even of the jokers themselves—the tortoise.   He appears
under that name in the translation of the bushman's tales;
he is, of course, Uncle Remus's Brer Tarrypin and he has
no less credit in South American stories.   Why is the tortoise
credited with such wisdom ?   One wonders. . . .   Is it
just this—that the bright little up-looking head and eyes,
when put forth, suggested the idea of intelligence ?   It is
something of a serpentine head and we have read a piece
of folklore which tells us that the serpent was the most subtle
of all the beasts of the field.

Surely the meaning of the tortoise symbol, stumbled
upon thus unexpectedly, goes far to explain the
difficulty.   To the native mind the ' serpentine head,'
appearing between the walls of shell, as naturally
pictures the clitoris as does the serpent its male
counterpart.   By a train of thought not difficult to
follow, this particular part of the body has grown to
symbolise femininity in general.   For Africans, therefore, tortoise stands for the feminine qualities of
persuasion—sometimes, perhaps, not untinged by
guile—as opposed to the more forceful male attributes.
It may be remembered that, in Pliny's day, a powder
made of a whole tortoise shell was thought to be an
aphrodisiac.

A few days later, in an Mbari house close to Okpala
market-place, the two emblems, snake and tortoise,
were found modelled side by side in the very centre
of the first row of symbolic figures.   Further on at
Obogwe, where the Mbari house is built in two
separate sections—the first, dedicated to the Thunder

God Amade Onhia, usually contracted into Amad-on-gha, and the second to his spouse, the Earth Goddess Ale or Ala—the phallic serpent was found in a position of great prominence in the shrine of the male deity, while tortoise was seen, modelled alone, in that of the goddess. Another example in which the two symbols were found, this time again in juxtaposition, was upon the main post of the shrine of the Juju Ogboloma at

FIG. 2. Phallic serpent (Eke) and tortoise (Naba), Okpala.

FIG. 3. Chief juju at Tema.

Tema near Degama—one of the principal Kalabari Jujus. Here, as so often, the two are combined with the figure of the sacred crocodile.[1]

With the new suggestion in mind, the detailed drawing of the sacred drum was examined, with the result that the emblems carved thereon seemed to take upon themselves a deeper significance. As already mentioned, at either end of the trough-like base, sits a male or female figure carved from the solid wood and distinct from the drum. To the left, the male, bearing

[1] See also figures on the ancestral tablet described on p. 121.

the symbols of manly strength, the sword in the one hand and the horn, typifying plenty and masculine virility, in the other. To the right the Mother—her head adorned with the high coiffure which, among Ibo, designates pride in offspring—a babe in her outstretched arms. In the centre of the drum itself, in the place of honour, carved in bold relief, is shown the phallic serpent. To the left of its pointed head rises the crescent moon—the world-wide symbol of growth—especially connected with childbirth, since expectant mothers count their time by its waxing and waning.

On either side, in the one case above and on the other below, are seen, twice repeated, the disputed signs, in both cases in conjunction with the old Cretan symbol of the union of the sexes—the double-headed axe. That the native explanation of the last-named figure was given in good faith, there is no reason to doubt. It is only another case of the way in which a symbol has survived long after the loss of its meaning. Indeed, a certain similarity exists; but, to those acquainted with native ways, I venture to think that the sharpness of angle marked in the joining of haft to head, instead of the easy curves called for by a representation of the musical instrument, is clear enough indication that the carver was following faithfully, though blindly, in the footsteps of long dead craftsmen whose work once bore another significance. A considerable number of examples of the old Minoan double-headed axe cult were found in other parts of West and Central Africa.

Besides those already discussed, only three other symbols are shown on the front of the great drum: viz. (1) the sacred crocodile—the terrible emblem of West Coast cults such as the Human Alligator Society and the great Ekoi women's secret cult of the Nature Goddess Nimm. Possibly the crocodile sometimes symbolises another plane of being or the future life; it is a common belief here that many souls live in crocodile form both during the life, and after the death, of the human body. There may also be some connection with the Egyptian worship of this creature. (2) The horn placed beneath the double-headed axe, as the so-called tortoise symbol is above—considered so powerful an emblem of virility that even its representation in bronze is supposed to excite desire, and, held in the hand of a pregnant woman, to assist delivery; and (3) the figure of a dog—regarded among Ibo and Kalabari as the means of first bringing fire to earth—possibly typifying the brute creation in general, or at least that part of it which is friendly to man.

Among some tribes, especially the Ekkett Ibibio, the tortoise shell is looked upon as the symbol of the Earth Deity, the goddess of fertility. The snake is the chief phallic symbol, not only on account of its shape but also because many species live underground and are therefore taken to represent the dead, to whose influence the fruitfulness of the crops is in many places considered mainly due.

II

MBARI HOUSES

FROM Aba, we passed through Omo Dim, in Owerri District, to visit the Mbari house there.

According to Ababua, priest of Amade Onhia at Ibo near Okomoko, the meaning of the word Mbari is ' fine ' or ' decorated.'

The central part of the strange structure at Omo Dim proved to be a rectangular building with steeply pointed roof and overhanging eaves, the latter so wide as to make a broad verandah.   The walls, forming the central chamber, were painted with elaborate frescoes, mostly in red and white upon yellow, or red and yellow upon white.   On either side of the main entrance to the inner, sacred apartment were here, and in most Mbari houses subsequently visited, figures so strikingly like those of Omogwa and Otammelli, the two strangely elongated guardians of the Thunderer's shrine at Ibodo,[1] as to make it probable that all had a common origin and were set there for the same purpose, namely to warn trespassers from approaching the shrine.

To others the people had only answered vaguely in reply to questions as to the purpose of the building: ' We make it for nothing, only to please ourselves.' The identity of the white figure at the top of the ladder

[1] See p. 45.

FIG. 4.   Outside the Mbari house, Omo Dim

was explained, as a portrait of the District Commissioner!

We were more fortunate, mostly on account of the energy displayed by the interpreter, Chief G. A. Yellow, a man of unusual intelligence, to whom the reason of our enquiries had been explained and who was far-sighted enough to wish to aid them by every means in his power. By his persuasion an old chief was induced to come forward and give somewhat more information. According to his account the name of the structure was Njokku Mbari, and it was erected in honour of a great ancestor, long dead, named Njokku and his wife Mbafor. The white figure at the top of the ladder on the right of the building represented Njokku himself and, as the chief artlessly pointed out, the birds upon the rungs of the ladder showed that this was the road by which the spirit of the dead man had climbed to his place in the sky, whence he now ruled as a great chief. The fact that he was painted white signified that he was no longer an earth child but had passed to the ghost realm, from whence he watched over his descendants who brought offerings at certain times of the year in order that he might be gently disposed towards them and grant plentiful harvests. As mentioned elsewhere, there is little doubt that the word Njokku is the same as that in use on the Nile, where Jok is the Dinka appellation for ancestral spirits and the Lango name for God.

On the testimony of a considerable number of Ibo we learned that no Mbari house is built save at the

orders of, and in honour of, one of the great deities
worshipped throughout the Etche country and Owerri
District, namely Ala, Amade Onhia, Otaminni (the
genius of the Otaminni River) called, by the priest
of his principal shrine at the Etche town of Opioro,
' The Lover of Ale,' and Oloba, a spirit living in the
Owerri bush.   So far as we could hear, the cult of the
latter is quite local.

The more than life-sized figure, facing the principal
entrance to the enclosure, was explained by the same
chief as that of the ancestress Mbafor, with her small
girl-piccan on her knee.   It was, he said, the head
priest of Ale, the Earth Goddess, whose shrine is
close to the Mbari house, who ordered the erection of
the building, chose out those who were to raise it and
himself directed every detail of decoration.   There
seemed, however, reason to believe that the figures of
the so-called ancestors Mbafor and Njokku really
represented Ale and Amade Onhia, regarded, in many
parts, as consorts and jointly responsible for the crops.
The resemblance between the figures of the deities, as
here shown, and those admittedly meant to depict the
Earth Goddess and Thunder God in other Mbari
houses, is so striking as surely to be more than a mere
matter of coincidence.

It is indicative of the position of Ale that only the
head chief of a town can aspire to become her priest.
This is the case with all dominant Jujus; for instance,
Otaminni at Opioro and Amade Onhia at Ozozo, the
parent shrine of the Thunder God's worship, from
which all other centres of the cult derive their power

FIG. 5. Clay figure of Ale in an Ibo Mbari house

The following was the account given by the Omo Dim chief as to the erection of the Mbari house:

'At the time of the new yam harvest the building is begun and, throughout the first part of the dry season, men and women, chosen for the purpose by the priest of Ale, work hard at beautifying and adorning it.' Only those specially designated for this purpose may take part. Should anyone not called thereto by the priest attempt to share in the work, death would fall upon such unauthorised intruders as surely as that which overtook him who, of old, stretched forth a presumptuous hand to the Ark.

Before the making of new farms the house must be finished and ready for the celebration of its strange rites. Later, when the germs of the new season's crop—corn-grains, sections of yam-tubers and seeds of pumpkins, great and small—have been confided to the dark bosom of Mother Earth, men and maids of the region gather together bringing gifts, 'rack upon rack of dried fish, goats, sheep and fowls without stint, palm-wine in plenty and all else needed for a great feast.' Of the maids, who have undergone initiatory ceremonies, a certain number are chosen by the Ezale (head priest of Ale) to act as priestesses for the rites about to be held in and around the Mbari shrine.

As to the nature of the ceremonies, the natives were naturally reluctant to speak ; but Mr. Whitehouse, a former District Commissioner, in a short account published in the *Journal of the African Society*,[1] declares

[1] 1904, pp. 134, 135.

them to have been of licentious character. Subsequent
enquiries confirmed this, and the nature of the rites is
borne out by the groups of clay figures set both round
the central shrine and beneath the roof depending
from the inner side of the wall, which encircles the
whole erection cloister-wise. These images represent,
with remarkable fidelity, the life-cycle of bird, beast
and human being, from the act of procreation—
depicted with astounding naïveté—to the lying down,
when life is done, for a last long rest in the arms of the
Earth Mother.

It is noticeable that, though beasts of prey play a
great part in the series, as is only natural under the
conditions here prevalent—such, for instance, as
leopard or hippopotamus devouring human beings—
these fierce beasts are shown either as destroyers or
as falling beneath the weapons of the hunters, never
in the propagation of their kind. Harmless or useful
creatures, on the other hand, such as fowls, both wild
and domesticated, dogs, sheep,[1] etc., together with
human beings, are depicted first in the act of procreation, secondly that of giving birth, thirdly suckling
their young and later in every conceivable scene of
life. Men are modelled as engaged in hunting,
fishing, canoeing—as police, court messengers, clerks
or musicians. Women are shown grinding cam-wood,
arranging elaborate coiffures, undergoing operations
of extreme delicacy from native doctors—every act

---

[1] In the Mbari houses of the neighbourhood of Omo Akani,
Owerri District, where the Juju Ogugu holds sway, monkeys also are
shown in the act of procreation.

of life indeed from cradle to grave, and even beyond, here finds itself reproduced.

The following account of the raising of an Mbari shrine was given by Amuneke of Umo Yekki quarter, Owerri:

There are many such houses in our part, and they are starting to make a new one, in honour of Ala, this month (October 1915) in my own quarter. First of all, when she, Amad'ongha or Otaminni, wish for a new house, they send a messenger called Abara.[1] This is a sort of devil, very dreadful to see! In his hand he carries a sword, because he is not only the messenger but also the executioner of Ala. The image at Omo Dim is made with birds perched upon the four horns on his head to show that he is of the Sky People and is often sent by Amad'ongha. The grasses in his hand show that he is also a servant of Ala.

He goes straight to the compound of the head chief (who is always priest of one of the four great cults already mentioned). Ordinary people are not able to see him; only Juju people can do this, but all hear the place shake as he enters. So soon as the chief knows, from this shaking, that the messenger has come, he sends to a native doctor who goes into the little shrine, where he talks to the spirits, and starts to beat drum. This is a sign to Abara that he is ready to hear the message. When the devil appears, the Juju man sees him clearly, listens to the commands he brings and reports them to the people, saying: 'The Juju asks for an Mbari house to be begun on such and such a day.' Then the head chief chooses out those who are to do the work, four men and three women from each compound. These go out secretly at night time so that no man may see them. If a strong Juju orders an Mbari house to be built and the people

---

[1] A different word to Abara 'Juju.'

do not obey at once, then at least twenty men from that quarter will die.

Before beginning to build, they make a high fence round the place so as to hide up the work they are going to do.

FIG. 6. Abara, the Messenger of Ale and Amad'ongha or Otaminni

Then they start to make a long house, called Eki-Wari,[1] in which to sleep. Across the middle of this a line is drawn.

[1] Our informant did not know of any link, yet it seems not without significance that the phallic pillars, raised by maidens before marriage to ensure plentiful offspring, also bear the name of Eki. See chapter vii.

Men sleep on the one side and women on the other. It would be regarded as a very bad thing should a woman permit a man to approach her at this time.

From the moment of starting the work till it is quite finished, even if it lasts for a year, no one may go home again, save the one man chosen from each compound to fetch food every day. That is why four men are always chosen to every three women ; because one is needed to go backwards and forwards on ' chop palaver.'

During all the time that the workers live inside the fence, they are forbidden to eat coconut, palm-nuts or cassava. Only cooked yams and soup may be eaten. Also, they may never sleep at night time, only by day. This rule is made because no one must see them when they go out to get the clay from which the figures are formed. This must be taken from the centre of a white ant hill, softened with water and carefully kneaded. No other clay is permitted to be used. So soon as darkness falls, they must begin to work and keep on till just after sunrise.

When the building is finished, on a day appointed by the Juju, all people, whose sons or daughters have been working, make ready for a great feast. After nightfall, they go to the Mbari house bearing a new-made pot. This must be one never before used, filled to the brim with clear water. Also they carry a cock for every son and a hen for each daughter. All their kinsfolk follow them up to the fence which hides the workers. Only the fathers and mothers may go inside, while the rest of the people wait without. Each couple steps, one after the other, in order of rank, together with the priest, before the big Juju set in front of the main doors. There the Juju priest kills a fowl and mixes its blood with water in the new bowl. Then, with a small wooden spoon, he throws some upon the head of son or daughter and pours the rest upon the great image to whom manillas are also offered.

At this point the father says :

'Ubu anyi abiala. Bia ikpe ogu. Anyi
'Now we are coming. Come judge matter. We (*i.e.* between us)

agi oku awsaw ade pa. Anyi emena nhie icheri.
you words again are no(t). We have done things thought your.

Ubu anyi abiala bia ekpaw nwa anyi. Oku
Now we are coming come to take son our. Words

awsaw adr pa.'
again are no(t) (*i.e.* all is finished).'

After this the mother says (for a son):

'Ubu-laka nhie oma ka ega enyi anyi na nwam
'Now things good you are going to give us and son my

makana ihie oma onu oma onu nagi. Nam na
because (he has done) things good work good work for you. I and

dim na ji unwenne na omu umonu na ewu
husband (my) and yam I have and children I born and goats

mwenne nhie oma ka anyi ega anhu afor anhua.'
I have things good make (for) us go see year this coming.'

For a daughter the mother says :

'Aborolam nwam obi oma. Mejiea na mejieadia
'I am taking my child (with) mind good. Give gifts to her and gifts to her husband (for)

onu-ma ka. Aronona ge anyi. Mfu ga ezi ubu-laka
work good your. Have worked for you we. If (I) go out now

afu na nam nhie ojo.'
finished for me things bad.'

So soon as the last word 'ojo' has been spoken, the priest seizes son or daughter and pushes him, or her, towards the parents who at once catch hold on either hand. All three *walk backwards* towards the gate. As the first foot strikes the threshold, they face round and the relatives waiting outside catch up the worker without an instant's delay and bear him back to his home. No foot of any such may be set to ground, lest Ala should be vexed.

When they reach the house all join in a great feast, with fish of every kind, plenty beef and tombo too much! That night the people tear down the fences, which were put up to hide the work, and burn them in a very great fire.

Those years, in which a new house is built, the yams grow bigger in our farms, goats and sheep have more piccans, while nearly always the girls chosen by the Juju for her work bear babes fine past those of other mothers. Usually they conceive soon after the work is finished—often within one or two moons of the play.

About every five or six years a new Mbari house is raised to Ala. She has more than any other god. Next in number come those built for Amade Onhia and still less for Otaminni and Oloba. I have never heard of any such house being made for the ancestors, as was said to be the case at Omo Dim. This may be true for that part ; only I know nothing of it.

It is in the little inner room that the god lives. In each of these a tall stone, shaped like an Ibudu, is set. After making its face smooth and clean all about, they cover it with a piece of white cloth. It is into this stone that the spirit enters.

Suppose one man charges another with doing bad things. Then they bring the accused for night time and lock him up alone in the small inner room. Next morning, if he be innocent, he walks forth unharmed; suppose he be guilty, then Juju kills him and his dead body is carried out at dawn. Perhaps Juju beat him to death, perhaps kill him other way; but always he die. No help for such man.

When a big pointed stone is found in our bush, an Mbari house is always built for it. In places where such things are, the knives, with which the old people made them, may be dug up out of the earth. I myself found one such knife at Baro. It was of very strong stone, hard past iron and curved over in a sharp point.

At Olakwaw near Owerri one very big stone was found. They carved it into an Ala figure and built a house for it. This they put in the place of honour, facing the big door. Also at Ne-Ewu and Ihuara in Owerri District there are stone

Fig. 8.   Humorous figures

Fig. 7.   Girl 'Mgbe, Otaminni house, Opioro

—

figures of Ala, Amad'ongha, Okpara Ala (the first born son of the Earth Goddess) and Eke, the great snake. This is the kind of big snake which lives for bush and always has a shining stone in its head, such as white people call diamond. It is because of these serpents that Eke day is said to take its name.

Images of Ale and Amad'ongha may be carved out of stone or moulded in clay, but must never be cut from wood like the Agu Isi (*i.e.* wooden images consulted by native doctors): for so the Juju orders. Ala has other sons beside Okpara Ala.[1] Among Etche Ibos and those of Owerri the younger sons are worshipped every month, four days after the coming of the new moon. They are represented under the shape of small cut stones such as were taken from the bad Onye Dibia (medicine man) at Awka. These stones are always kept in one of the round box stools, rubbed with cam-wood. The medicine man sits upon the box, then rises and shows the stones to the people who throw themselves upon the ground before these, praying for piccans, kids, lambs and yams. These sons are never represented in any other shape. No figures of them are to be found in Mbari houses.

Sometimes we call these buildings Mbari, sometimes 'Mgbe. This last word means a small boy or girl orphan. There are two kinds of 'Mgbe—those who have relatives to look after them and those who have none. We call the latter Osu 'Mgbe, *i.e.* the worst 'Mgbe. He is so very poor he can only get food by searching round the bush for palm nuts. For this reason his image is nearly always made with palm nuts in hand.

In olden days such a boy was always bought by one or other of the quarters and presented as a slave to the Juju. Afterwards he might never enter the compound which bought him, but could go to beg food from others. Sometimes, when he has grown big enough, he makes himself a

[1] At the Etche town of Okudu Mba there was an Mbari house erected in honour of Ajala (Aja ground or mud), 'a brother of Ale.'

little house in one of the corners of the Mbari. Then people bring yams to him. Sometimes too the Juju asks for chop for him. If the Juju loves him very much, it will also ask one of the chiefs to give him a slave wife; but such a boy may never marry any free-born girl of the town. The same rule holds for girl orphans bought with money and given to the Juju. They may take slave husbands, but never marry a free-born man.

Another figure to be seen in every Mbari house is that of the ape Ogbango. This is the kind into which the souls of bad Ibo go after death.

In the Western Etche country these temples are generally called 'Mgbe houses. Umoyo, the principal place hereabouts, is a queer little town—or rather two towns—through which runs a single long street, fenced in on either side by a palisade of posts and palm leaves. The houses lie well back, often out of sight from the main road, in gardens which bear luxuriant crops. At the end of the street stretches a line of cacti to keep out evil influences.

The head chief Wobilo was friendly to Government, and we had hoped to gain from him a considerable amount of information regarding the origin and rites of this singular cult. By an unfortunate accident, however, some of the principal men of the town had lately been drowned in the Juju water formed by the sacred Otaminni River just below its junction with the Ogochi. No sooner were the sad tidings made known to relatives and friends than the whole town turned against the head chief, saying that the deaths lay at his door, because he had induced them to undertake the journey which resulted in their untimely end.

Fig. 9.　Shrine of Otaminni, Opioro

In consequence, Wobilo found himself outcast in his own town and, when on our next visit we asked a few questions concerning the figures in the local 'Mgbe house, the chief refused to run the risk of increasing his unpopularity by giving away information, and we were everywhere met by the answer: ' I do not know. We did it for no reason. Perhaps our ancestors may have had knowledge of these things ; but, as for us, we have long since forgotten, and only copy the customs taught by our fathers because we believe that by so doing we shall draw prosperity upon our town.'

The only information we could get ran as follows:

> Mbari or 'Mgbe is our Chineke, also our Juju. People from Orata built the house. At certain seasons girls dress themselves and come before the shrine, there to dance, eat and drink.

> Amad'ongha is a great Juju, but our people do not worship him much. His proper country is over the other side of the Otaminni River.

When an Mbari house was to be erected in Etche country, a medicine man was consulted as to time and place of building. Thereupon he brought out a human skull—in the old days that of a slaughtered victim, but since the coming of white rule one sought amid the ' bad bush ' near his town. Round this were set out the Agu images—always, be it remembered those typifying fatherhood and motherhood, together with representatives of the animal kingdom, including ' dog ' who brought fire to earth. A cock was killed and its blood sprinkled over the skull and the little images. Then the magician gave utterance to the supposed wish of the Earth Mother or Sky Father with regard to the building to be erected in their honour, by means of which, it was thought, prosperity of farm, byre and marriage bed might be secured to the town.

At Opioro stands an Mbari house built in honour of the spirit of the Otaminni River—the only one known to us throughout the Division. The image of Otaminni is set in the centre of the front side, with his ' big relation ' Ala to his right and his three wives Ogori, Ocham and Wujere in a row on his left.

On the opposite side of the house, in the seat of honour, sits the Earth Mother again; while, near her, groups of women are engaged in pursuits set apart by custom as purely feminine. For instance, a mid-wife ushers a babe into the world; cam-wood is ground, etc. All the characters, with which one had grown familiar in other houses of this type, were here repro-duced with one exception, that of ape. An enquiry into the cause of his absence brought the surprised reply: ' Ogbango is here, sir! He stand for middle place at other side of house.'

A visit to the spot indicated revealed no sign of what we were seeking—only an unseemly group such as is to be found in nearly all such buildings, the woman bending forward at right angles from the waist, her head resting upon the square base of one of the roof pillars, while the male figure behind her was unmis-takably engaged in the Geschlechts Akt. The present head priest of Otaminni, Amade Onyeche, was at the moment anxious to be appointed to the post of warrant chief in the place of his late brother. This

Fig. 10.   The Chief of Opioro, head priest of Otaminni

made him not only willing but eager to impart information. His disclosures were, indeed, on certain points
rather embarrassingly full. He stated, and his account
was afterwards borne out by those of other Ibo, that
the male figure was not that of a man but of the very
Ogbango whom we had thought absent. In proof
of this statement the priest pointed out that, in its right
hand, on the left shoulder and beneath the left arm,
the ape held a round ball, representing those hard
fruits which, according to widespread native testimony,
it is his habit to fling at passers-by, thereby stunning,
or even killing, them. This we had already heard
from many parts of the country. At Obogwe it was
added that so heavy were the fruits and so great the
strength of this ape that it was thought he might even
succeed in stunning an elephant therewith ! Amade
Onyeche continued:

> It is customary among our people to take up the position
> of this couple for such a purpose, when there is no bed near
> at hand. It is forbidden to lie upon the ground, lest Ale
> should be defiled thereby. There are many of these great
> apes in our bush who, if they meet a woman alone, force
> her to bear a child to them.

The same belief, according to Amuneke of Umo
Yekki, is held in the neighbourhood of Owerri. It is
probably connected with the idea that the souls of bad
men pass into ape form at death. It appears that the
evil human spirit, confined in the animal body, is
thought to take this means of providing a new form in
which to re-incarnate.

III

MBARI HOUSES (*continued*)

In Mbari houses built in honour of Amade Onhia it is made perfectly clear, as is natural, that the Thunderer himself holds first place, while his consort is of secondary importance. In the shrine at Omo Dim, as previously mentioned, the place of honour, facing the entrance, was occupied by the figure of the so-called deified ancestress Mbafor—a bowl for offerings sunk into the ground at her feet and her daughter upon her knee. The face and form of the mother are bright yellow, the colour of the clay from which she is modelled as are those of Ala in all shrines yet visited; while the whole body of the child is dead white, like that of the Thunderer himself, the deified ancestor Njokku seated above his sky ladder, or indeed ghosts and ' sky people ' in general.

On the white of her body five coal-black crescent moons had been painted; one just above the shoulder, one on the top of the arm and three down the flank. All, save that on the arm, showed a protuberance in the centre, exactly in the place where the nose would come when children draw the face of the man in the moon. The point would not have been worth mentioning but for the fact that in each Mbari house visited a peculiar decoration was noticeable, only to be described as a screen of lattice-work, formed of

Fig. 11. Figure of Mbafor in the Njokku Mbari at
Omo Dim

interlacing human figures. This was explained as representing the slaves sacrificed and flung into the grave—or laid there still living, but with broken arms

and thigh bones—to form carpet and bier for the body of the dead chief. It may well have borne some such interpretation, but this would hardly explain the fact that, in each case which we came across, one row of figures, usually the centre one, bore faces the shape of a crescent moon, mostly dead white and outlined by a deep black rim. At Omo Dim, Okpala and Obogwe too there is a figure —which is duplicated with more or less fidelity in several other shrines and which for obvious enough reasons was named, by my companions, ' little moon-face '—of the same type as those in the human trellis work.

Fig. 12. "Little Moon-face," Omo Dim

Now the crescent moon is a sign of growth the world over. Ekoi women come together, beneath her faint beams, to carry out the rites which, according to their belief, will ensure fruitfulness. Ibibio and Ibo also hold that her rays are endued with fecundative powers, while pregnant women count the time to their delivery by her waxing and waning.

Some few weeks later, in passing through the town of Ebubu in the extreme east of Degama District inhabited by that strange and hitherto unstudied tribe, the Mbolli, we came across a shrine of a type such as we had never before seen. It is carved from a solid block of wood some four feet high, set in a carefully smoothed clay base, swathed round the bottom by folds of white cloth and surmounted by an inverted crescent. The name of this Juju is Obo Esa, *i.e.* in Mbolli dialect four hundred yams. The reason given for this name is that only full chiefs have the right to erect such a fetish, to which they must sacrifice each harvest-time baskets containing the given number of yams. It was explained that Obo Esa is a male Juju—a statement borne out by the appearance of the symbolic pillar—and to him, at the cutting of new farms and digging of fresh yams, living sacrifices must be brought and slain so that their blood is shed upon the clay base, whence it trickles down over the seven little moon-shaped depressions to the thirsty earth beneath. These small half moons may well typify the period during which the yams are confided to the bosom of Mother Ale—called Nkike by the Mbolli—while the great crescent, surmounting the pillar, probably represents that of the month of September during which the harvest festival is usually held.

Considering the close connection between the waxing moon and the powers of fertility, it is not without signi-ficance that personified representations of the crescent are to be found in each Mbari house, especially when it is remembered that the shrine of the Earth Goddess is always close by and that only after consultation with her priest is the building begun and carried through.

Again, although we were expressly told, as already related, that the chief figure at Omo Dim did not represent either of the principal deities, but only a deified ancestress, yet a man present volunteered the information—it is true, in a highly superior manner—that some old and very ignorant people held them to be those of Amad'ongha and Ale. So stupid, however, were such that they even believed the white child, on the knee of the Earth Mother, to be the moon! As if any but the most foolish could look upon the moon as a daughter of Earth!

In the Obogwe Mbari house—the only one which we have yet found built in two separate edifices—the first building was dedicated to Amad'ongha and the second to Ale, locally called Ala. Our informant, Omere Madu, was the son of the late head chief who therefore, *ipso facto*, was priest of Ale. He told us that this goddess was the dominant power in the town, and that she ordered her priest to have the two houses built in that place and form—one for herself and one for her spouse Amad'ongha. In both buildings he sits in the seat of honour, but in the first alone, while in the second she is seen on his left, in the same position as that of the figure at Obodo to which her name was first given, but which was later called Omu Ngwaw, the fruitful mother.[1]

[1] See p. 40.

In the temple dedicated to the Thunderer, on the left of the central figure is seen one, the name of which was said to be Eku Nechi—*i.e.* ' the big woman who cooks,' or more fully ' who gathers the children of others around her and cooks for them.' The figure is seated, supporting a boy and a girl against her sides ; while another pair sits, one upon each of her outstretched legs. The most singular thing about this group is that each of the male children bears a crescent moon for face, while from the necks of the two girls is painted a cloth thickly covered with white dots. On the wall of the Ale shrine, a fresco may be seen on which a moon-faced boy is depicted climbing up the right hand side of a rainbow, painted in black, yellow and red stripes. In such a position he is sup-

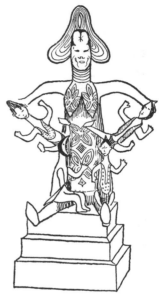

FIG. 13. Group in Obogwe Mbari house

posed to be an envoy from the Earth Goddess, climbing the sky with a message from Amade Onhia, or, when descending, bringing word from the latter to the children of men. Beneath, on a black ground, a crescent moon and stars are shown—the stars represented by white dots exactly like those painted round the necks of the girl piccans of Eku Nechi. It is not

impossible therefore that here again, in ' the big woman
who feeds the children of others,' we have another
forgotten picturing of Ale, the Earth Mother, with her
starry progeny.

A singular fact about all the Mbari shrines hitherto
visited is that, in each, figures may be seen, obviously
modelled with the express intention of depicting
licence in its most blatant form. Primitive peoples
the world over, however frank in picturing or
mentioning facts treated with the greatest reticence
by civilised races, are usually ignorant of real vulgarity
or indecency, since the very simplicity of manner and
treatment robs their statements of offence. The
Ibo of this region, especially, have a code with
regard to sexual matters which, however lax according to our ideas, is yet strangely strict in some direc-
tions. According to them four of the most evil things
are:

(1) For man and woman to lie together on the earth,
since this is thought to defile Ale. Among Kalabari
indeed the idea is carried so far that no woman is
allowed, under any circumstances, to seat herself
upon the ground. In the absence of stool or con-
venient tree-trunk she must stand. As already mentioned, according to chief Amade Onyeche, the position
adopted by Etche Ibo, when no bed, mat or cloth
is available, is for the woman to stand bending forward
at right angles from the waist, while her lover stands
immediately behind.

(2) Connection is absolutely forbidden during the
hours of daylight, or even at night time when a light

is burning in the room; also at any time in the bush or in a farm, where there is no house.

(3) It is the height of impropriety for a man to have relations with a woman who is not clothed in the prescribed custom.

(4) For a husband to attempt to view the genital organs of his wife is regarded as so serious an offence as to be considered valid ground for divorce. In a case brought before me in the Degama Native Court, the claim ran: ' To demand freedom of marriage on account of peeping.'

In every Mbari house yet visited, however, figures were seen modelled with the obvious purpose of expressing a breach of one or other of these rules. In most of the buildings groups were found in which the feminine figure was shown partially lying on the ground—in a position impossible to any human anatomy and therefore, it would seem, so posed as intentionally to express direct rebellion against the generally accepted rules of decency.

An official of high rank, who was the first Government representative to visit this region, described to me a shrine which he saw about twelve years ago, near Ingaw in Owerri District, where certain points were even more naïvely depicted than by those erected in the present day. Among the more noticeable groups were men in the act of copulating with a sheep and antelope respectively. As regards the latter animal, it is not without interest to recall that, according to several accounts from well-informed sources, ancient Yoruba custom ordained that, after the kill of his first antelope, a young hunter must have connection with the still warm form. Possibly some such rule obtained, or maybe even yet exists, in these regions.

The group of men and sheep seems to point to the existence of a like custom among Ibo as one learns, on good authority, prevails among the neighbouring Ijaw, with whom the chief feature of male initiatory rites consists in each boy proving his manhood, before a circle of elders, upon a specially selected sheep. Should he be unsuccessful, he must wait until the following year and is prevented from marriage until after having passed the test. From certain information it would appear that one of the principal centres, where this rite is carried out, may be found on a southern creek in the neighbourhood of Kula.[1] It was naïvely added that the sheep 'never go 'gree to this and always vex too much' when the rite was carried out. Later, a similar custom was reported from among the Ekkpahians of Ahoada District.

It is true that every Ibo or Kalabari who mentioned the subject was eager to state that Ekkpahians perform this rite 'merely out of badness; for no proper reason at all.' Yet, though it is unfortunately not permitted me to give a single name as authority, it would appear, after very careful weighing of evidence, that the practice has been exacted from time immemorial as a test of manhood. Both Ibo and Kalabari also

[1] In this neighbourhood are the principal shrines of Adumu, the head and father of all the snake cults of the region. The little village of Adum-Ama is its chief centre, while at 'Ngeri-Baw-Ama it was stated that 'only men may talk with him; for with his cult some of the most important of the male secrets are said to be connected.'

asserted that unnatural vice is *homosexuality (?)* extensively practised among this people, though rare with other races of the Division; but it is only just to state that the practice appears to be carried on not for the purpose of sensual indulgence, but, in some cases at least, from the idea, held among certain Australian tribes, that such customs increase the race by magical means.

That the practice is not held in as great detestation throughout Ekkpahian and neighbouring territory as among other tribes is proved by the more or less casual manner in which the matter was mentioned as well as from one or two Court cases. It will be enough to quote that heard at Omokku on January 20th, 1913, in which Atoma of Erema charged Okereke of Idu with indecent assault. In the course of her evidence plaintiff stated on oath:

> About three months ago accused came to my father's house to have connection with him. At that time I went to bed. . . .
>
> *Question by Court.* When he came to your house, where did he stay with your father to have connection?
>
> *Answer.* Outside the house.
>
> *Question by Accused.* What date did I come to your house?
>
> *Answer.* Orie day.
>
> *Question by Court (to father).* Was accused your friend?
>
> *Answer.* No.
>
> *Question by Court.* Did accused ever come to your house and have connection with you at night?
>
> *Answer.* Yes. He always come to my house and prosecutor saw him.

Among Ekkpahians and the Abuan, as well as with the Western Ikwerri, elaborate, two-storied buildings may be seen, upon which the wealth and utmost resources of the town have been lavished, even to stained- and patterned-glass for all the windows. My attention was drawn to these buildings by a man high in the medical service of the Protectorate, with the information that they were erected for the practice of unnatural vices. This was later confirmed from native sources with the addition that they were the homes of the Obukere Club and that the customs were of religious significance. The fact that such habits exist is, unfortunately, too well known to be worth mentioning, were it not for a few words dropped by one of the chiefs and intended in extenuation of the practice. ' It is true,' he said, ' that the custom is a very bad one ; yet aged men tell us that it was taught in olden days as a very great magic *whereby our flocks and herds might be multiplied and made strong. Even, it is said, the crops in the farms are increased thereby.*'

The idea was confirmed by another chief who however insisted that it was only a tradition from the olden time—held by dead men, very far away—and he did not think that any such belief was prevalent nowadays. He also added, cautiously, that this form of vice was far less indulged in at present than was formerly the case.

The information fitted in with that already gleaned concerning the supposed efficacy of phallic shrines set up amid the fields in order to secure plentiful crops.

As a result, further information was sought concerning the cult of Obukere, one of the most interesting of whose lodges was discovered at Obelle Oduaha. An avenue, half a mile in length, every trunk of which bore a sinister-looking smear of cam-wood dye, led to the house. At the entrance to this grove it opens out into a cleared space, from the centre of which springs a clump of trees smeared with deep bands of red and hung round with white cloth. Behind these rises a giant ant-hill, while round their roots a mound of earth about five feet high was piled. Amid the rich mould and fallen leaves stood votive pots and bowls, among which bundles of young tombo palms just bursting from the parent kernels, were to be seen, mostly enclosed in wrappings of broad green leaves bound round with tie-tie. This clump of trees is regarded as the abode of Obukere himself. Here members of his cult assemble to carry out the rites. Before his dwelling-place the worshippers cover their faces and, thus veiled or masked, go in procession through the sacred grove—the tree trunks of which, down to the smallest sapling, have been fresh smeared with the symbolic blood-red cam-wood. In these regions Obukere is regarded as the great giver of fertility to all in air, water or upon earth—fish, animals, plants or men.

All lodges of this club as yet visited show a peculiar development in the highly conventionalised animal head-dresses which are worn for plays. In the Otu Obukele (house of Obukele or Obukere) a big shed made of solid wooden posts, at the Abuan town of

Okobaw, some head-dresses of unusual type were found; among them representations of antelopes, porcupines and the 'increase of the Sky people,' typifying the sky world above that of men.

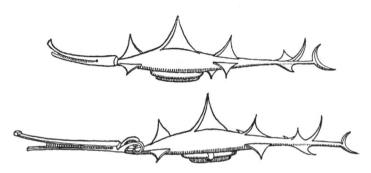

Fig. 14. Obukere Club head-dresses

Round the lodge at Obelle Oduaha were seven phallic shrines six of which were of the usual pillar type, while the seventh showed a featureless head, arms and legs indicated in the roughest manner, and only the distinctly feminine organs modelled with any care. The position of these shrines in close proximity to the house of Obukere worshipped with the avowed purpose of increasing fertility in man, animals and crops, can hardly be regarded as without significance. Within the house were two objects of interest—a xylophone in the shape of a canoe manned by eight figures, stated by the chief to have been specially designed to express 'joy' and raise feelings of pleasure in those who behold them; and an object which strongly resembled the Ajokko Ji or king yam shown to us at Oppe, separated by the sacred crocodile swamp from Alessa, and which will be more fully described later on page 99.

The drum used at Oduaha to call together the members of the Obukere Club was said to have been brought from Abua and to have been made for the Sekapu Club, connected with the spirits of fish, crocodiles and—in this part of the world—land beasts. It may be only a whim of the carver that the figure of the woman, depicted with rounded body as a sign of pregnancy, should be joined to that of the sacred crocodile. Drums of similar type were later found among Abaw Ibo.

FIG. 15. Sacred drum used to call together
the Obukere Club, Oduaha

IV

MBARI HOUSES (*continued*)

In nearly all towns of importance in the Etche country, elaborate Mbari shrines are to be found, built in honour of the Thunder God. In most, just within the principal entrance, may be seen the seated figure of the deity, white from head to foot, and bearing in the right hand a sword, spear or bayonet, and in the left an imitation of one of the old stone axe-heads, thought by natives to be thunder bolts, or one of the long iron sceptre-rattles, or possibly another sword or dagger. By his side sits his consort, to whom various names are given, most of them apparently synonyms for the Earth Goddess Ale, Ala, Ana or Aja. At Ibodo we were told by one informant that the figure represented Ala—Bride of the Bladed Thunder. The more general Ibo idea as to her identity was confided by the head priest, Achongwa by name, to chief G. A. Yellow: ' That,' said he, ' is Omu Ngwaw, wife of Amad'ongha.'

Omu Ngwaw is literally ' the children (or young leaves) of the tombo palm tree,' *raphia vinifera*. Now, when a woman has given birth to a first or second babe, the days which she spends in seclusion are often called by the same name, while the word for fruitfulness itself, or giving birth, is Omumu. The connection thought to exist in primitive minds is the probable reason why young palm leaves are in such evidence

FIG. 16.   Figure in Mbari House, Umoyo

FIG. 17.   Wrestling scene ('Mba) in shrine of Amade Onhia
and Ale.   Shrine drummers on the right

before the shrines of all beneficent Jujus; the half-unfolded frond stands as type and symbol of fruitful motherhood.

On floor and walls, serpents twine and twist ; hippopotami hold men half devoured in their mouths, leopards stand over new-slain goats, elephants wave long trunks or fall to the guns of hunters, apes climb or swing, and fabulous creatures disport themselves on every hand. A clerk counts his money on a little table. Two wrestlers may be seen locked in one another's arms [1] and a native doctor anoints the womb of a woman patient with a feather dipped in oil. In short, so far as in them lies, the whole life-history of the people is here reproduced with infinite pains and care. As in the Owerri Mbari houses, the head-dresses of the women are most elaborately rendered, while the modelling of a ram's head and of one small monkey which sat devouring a corn-cob were extraordinary samples of artistic skill. Again, a peculiar feature of several of these were figures obviously modelled with the intention of expressing the feeling of joy. It is probably only a coincidence that so many of the figures of Ale show much enlarged navels—the ὀμφάλος of the Earth Goddess.

In all these shrines the mural decoration is not painted, but applied to the walls like a gigantic piece of Cloisonné—clay, tinted with various dyes, being filled in between strips of raphia palm which serve to

---

[1] The wrestling scene depicted in every Mbari house generally represents the ceremonial wrestling ' to help the crops grow ' described on p. 112 *et seq.*

outline the design exactly as does the brass edging the enamelled leaves and flowers of the above-mentioned ware.

One of the most interesting of the temples visited lay some two and a half miles off the main road near Ibodo and was approached first by a narrow bush-path and later by a broad way over-arched by great trees, the branches of which interlaced overhead to form a clear translucent twilight even at noonday. As we passed beneath the fern-fringed, orchid-decked boles, the sky was overcast and the sun already low in the west, while the voice of the Thunder God might be heard in the distance—a low, threatening note in the twilight.

When the village of Omako was reached and we approached the shrine, the sun was just setting. Blue smoke rose from amid the strange figures, over which flames flickered and danced from a little fire tended by an old, old woman, who among such uncanny surroundings was quietly cooking her evening meal. She was the ' slave of the Juju ' who had sought his protection as a refuge from oppression untold moons ago. Her whole life is spent amid the weird figures which she guards and serves, lighting fires during the rains that the soft clay may not be melted nor the roof and wood-work rotted by damp and mould—though, strangely enough, it is strictly forbidden to make the slightest attempt at repairing when cracks appear in figure or wall, however much care was expended on the building of the shrine.

So near to one another are the figures that the little sleeping mat of the attendant could hardly find space

FIG. 18.   Clay figure of Amade Onhia in an Ibo Mbari house

to be stretched out in between. Their eyes were set with fragments of looking-glass, which twinkled and gleamed in the most life-like way, as the flames rose and fell. How many years the gentle old slave, with her soft voice and deprecatory gestures, had served the Juju, none could tell. She herself seemed to have lost all memory of any other life ; but the dim eyes brightened at the gift of tobacco leaves and the gentle voice followed us, still calling Ndeawo—the common word both for ' thanks ' and for ' greeting '—as we went away.

In every case which we have seen as yet, the Thunder God wears a sharply pointed black beard. In many instances little rattles hang from his neck or are attached to a spear or staff held in his hand, while a cluster of bells is slung from a rope usually passing over the right shoulder and resting on the left hip. In one place his feet were set upon a curved bar of iron which had once been gaily painted and was said to represent the rainbow. It is with the rattles that he produces the roll of his thunder, while the bells strike together to form the clash and bang of each separate peal. The type of figure was identical with that of the so-called deified ancestor Njokko, seated at the top of his sky ladder upon each rung of which ' air people,' *i.e.* birds, were perched.

It is perhaps not without significance that, upon either hand of his throne, two slender pillars the shape of an elongated torch and each bearing a bird, are set.[1] These are small and vaguely modelled, but it is

[1] Cf. The Bird and Pillar Cult of old Crete.

possible that they once represented the eagles of Zeus
—which, among Ibibio, are still sacred to Obumo, the
Thunderer.[1]

At Ibodo, on either side of the door of the central
shrine—the ' holy of holies ' which only the priest
can enter unscathed—we first noticed the two strangely
shaped figures which are also to be seen guarding the
inner sanctuary of the Owerri Mbari houses.   They
were thus explained to us:

' These are the servants of Amad'ongha.   Their
names are Omogwa and Otamelli.   The first '—with
spread tresses—' is calling up the tempest by striking
on her mouth.'   (This action was later described, at
another shrine, as ' cleaning her teeth with a bush
stick! ')   ' The second is about to loosen her hair
which floats around her in the storm-wind darkening
all the earth '—a possible picturing of the rain-bearing
clouds.

Omogwa's left hand is stretched out to warn intruders
from entering the chamber which she and her sister Alose
are set to guard, lest thereby the wrath of Amade Onhia
should be drawn down upon the trespasser.

In former days, when men had offended against the law of
the Juju, they were brought by the priests and shut up within
the shrine.   Then, in the night time, came some fearful
thing to torture them to death, perhaps by beating, perhaps
in other ways.   At any rate the body of the offender was
always borne forth at dawn and shown to the trembling
people as a sign of the fate which would overtake any who
dared disobey the law of the Thunder God or the commands
of his priests.

[1] See *Life in Southern Nigeria.*

Fig. 19. The Guardians of the Shrine, Omogwa and Otamelli

As already mentioned on page 20, this custom also prevailed among the people of Owerri. Near the two Alose, on each side of the inner entrance, are small holes in which offerings of kola are placed when people come to ' bless the shrine ' or ask for special favours.

In the neighbourhood of Ibodo and indeed all over the Etche country, according to the testimony of chief Achongwa, it is customary before cutting palm-nuts to offer sacrifice to some specially tall trees, one of which will be found in every compound. These are named Amad'ongha's palms, because the people say that those, which reach very high, are nearer to the deity. Men who neglect this rite find that their palm-nuts do not produce much oil. Later, we found that the custom was also practised by Aro and a row of the trees—here known as the palms of Kamalo, the name given by this people to Amad'ongha—was shown us in the compound of chief Ogunda at Azu-Miri near Nkarahia. In an Aro compound at Ozoaba each tree had a tall palm-leaf tied against its base, the top leaflets cut off straight and surmounted by a scarlet parrot's feather, an egg, etc.

At Ibodo, from the Thunderer's shrine to the corner of the rest-house, stretches a sacred grove beneath the shade of which native pots and other offerings may be found. Here, during the dry season, a number of small mats of plaited palm were seen, each bearing an offering of goat's flesh. It is perhaps worth mentioning that, among Ibibio, curtains of plaited palm-leaf are hung before holy pools and groves or round the trunks of sacred trees. The plaited part is said to represent the rainbow, while the long fringe from the lower edge typifies the rain itself.

In the grove at Ibodo beneath one of the trees, peeled, short-branched wands—the symbol of lightning —were still standing, and we were told that formerly many such had been set up in other spots. When these rods decay, the power of the Thunder God is said to pass from them into the nearest tree. Once drawn within the many-forked branches, the ' mana ' of Amad'ongha fades not with the fading of its first frail tenement, but is drawn into the vegetation around, growing and spreading with each new season's boughs.

At the far end of the sacred grove stands a tree such as we had never seen elsewhere, of which the crowded panicles of single petaled flowers, deepest crimson in colour, swayed to and fro in the breeze amid dark quivering leaves, or fell earthward in showers, like drops of new drawn blood.

One night, at the beginning of the tornado season, we were sleeping in the neighbouring rest-house, when a storm arose with the appalling suddenness usual at this time of year. The wind tore at the frail palm-leaf roofs, while rain lashed in through open window- and door-frames, flash after flash was followed, with scarce an interval, by crash and roar so deafening that for a long time all other sounds were drowned in the awful tumult. As the storm began to pass away, another sound made itself heard in the lengthening intervals. Each lightning gleam was followed by a burst of trumpeting, as though the followers of the storm god had come together undaunted by the force of the tempest to hold a play in honour of their great deity. It is impossible to give any idea of the impressiveness of this act of worship. From out the impenetrable darkness, between long lines of rain, like a sword from its scabbard leapt the dazzling flash. The branches of the sacred grove moaned and swayed, bitumen dark against this more than daylight brilliance; while, from beneath their shade or from the neighbourhood of the shrine, each burst of flame was answered by a blare of savage trumpets, the sound of which merged into the roll of the sequent thunder.

So long as the storm lasted the strange music continued, broken now and again by the cries of the terrified cattle, which rose in chorus from countless byres and were hardly distinguishable at times from the rude horns blown by their owners.

Save for the fact that the outer colonnade, which gives accommodation to further groups of figures in Owerri Mbari houses, is absent, wholly or in part, from many of the Etche shrines, the buildings are practically identical in type. Many groups are to be found, save for the smallest of details, exactly reproduced in each, and it is owned that freedom of intercourse between the sexes is allowed in the cults of both Ale and Amade Onhia at certain seasons, with the idea that this will have the effect of increasing fruitfulness not only among the human inhabitants of the town but also in farm and byre.

The connection between the two cults was indicated by a practice which still obtains at Omo Chuku, a quarter of the town of Ibo near Okomoko inhabited by Etche Ibo. The principal chief of the place, Ababua by name, is also head priest of the Thunder God and, by the local law of the cult, is only permitted to eat in a hut which stands by itself in the middle of his compound. In this, all the dried yams and seed-corn are stored and there too is his Ajokko Ji or king yam, here represented by a basket filled with yams and skulls.

Each wife cooks in turn, and the one who has prepared the meal serves it and is permitted to partake. Should the priest so will, son or daughter may be invited to join in the repast; but none may do so without special permission. The chief himself sits upon an elaborately carved stool, but the others place themselves humbly upon the ground or on small logs. The doorway is curtained by a fringe of young palm-leaves which are never allowed to wither.

The son of chief Ababua, who accompanied us for some distance, stated that his father might never eat of the new season's yams for at least two months after this was permitted to ordinary men. As chief priest of Amad'ongha, Ababua was also obliged by ancient law to perform certain ceremonies to his personal god as well as to the special protectors among his ancestors—the shrines of which are placed just within the threshold of his Obiri (reception room)— before allowing any portion of the new season's yams or corn to pass his lips. It was explained that, by taking his food amid the seed set apart for planting, the priest was thought to endow these with special fertility by the power of the Thunderer whom he served.

Not far from the little dining hut, a small, highly decorated mud house was to be seen, consisting of a dark inner chamber opening from an outer porch-like one. The chief explained that this was the local Mbari house and that they built it each year—making the mud walls gay with shells and brightly coloured plates because their fathers had bidden them do this in order to draw down prosperity upon their people. He added, somewhat hastily, that no special rites were carried out and that the structure got its name only because the word means ' fine ' or ' decorated '—probably from its decorations or, perhaps, from the gay robes, beads and brass ornaments worn by the women when gathered together there.

All round the compound the much-branched, peeled wands sacred to Amad'ongha are to be seen. Beneath one of these, two pottery drums were placed, one half embedded in the ground and one above. By the principal shrine before the main entrance a curious adjunct was noticed. From a sapling, cut so as to form a fork, hangs a large oval calabash. Between the prongs a farm hoe is held, while beneath it two tortoises are impaled. The explanation of this given by the chief was that one night his god ordered them to be placed beside the shrine. The combination of objects, taken in conjunction with the fact that this priest of the Thunderer may only eat amid the seed corn and yams, suggests that this is another of the many Jujus for augmenting the fertility of the farm. It is not without significance that, beside that of

FIG. 20.   Burial scene in Amade Onhia shrine, Okehin

Amade Onhia, the only other shrine of importance in Omo Chuku is dedicated to Ale.

At Okehin, the Thunderer, instead of occupying a whole building, is only given the front verandah of a house. At one end was to be seen the figure of a mother with a new-born babe in her arms; at the other, a group representing a corpse laid in the grave with a pot of offerings beside it and a pet monkey watching at the foot by the seated figure of a woman. The pot of offerings usually contains a small plate, knife, pipe, tobacco, snuff and bottle of gin, rum or palm-wine. Between these two groups representing birth and death stands the figure of a medicine man, a magic horn in his right hand and a Juju knife in his left.

In niches cunningly contrived in the rear wall, or upon the low clay ridge which separates the verandah from the road, carefully modelled birds sit upon nests of interwoven twigs, containing eggs, tinted or speckled in close imitation of nature. Small monkeys climb the pillars, dogs mount guard, while the phallic serpent twines and twists between all.

V

SKY GOD AND EARTH GODDESS

AMONG Etche Ibo, especially those to the west of the Otaminni River, Amade Onhia has practically usurped the place of Chi, the Creatrix, and reigns as supreme deity. For months after our arrival, we were invariably told by natives of all parts of the Division that the Thunderer was distinct from his brother Igwe, Lord of the Bright Sky. Later on, while collecting information concerning rain-making by magical means, it transpired from the words of the invocation used that the two originally symbolised different aspects of the same personality—Zeus of the thunder, lightning and storm cloud, Lord of the dark sky as well as the bright. Now, though most people regard them as separate deities, the old idea has not yet died out, especially among rain-makers.

Formerly, it is said, Igwe was more generally worshipped than at present. This was explained as due to the fact that the God of the Bright Sky only gives advice by his oracles and does not ensure wealth, health or special good fortune to his votaries; while these additional gifts may be obtained through prayer to Amade Onhia.

In January 1915 good fortune led us to Ozozo, where stands the greatest of all shrines of the Thunder God—a temple not made with hands—the sanctity of which is so great that pilgrims come thither from hundreds of miles. Until now its existence had been carefully guarded from the knowledge of Europeans, and the chief priest had so far avoided coming into contact with any white man of the few who had visited the neighbourhood.

Early next morning we set out to seek the place of pilgrimage. The way led through a part of the bush set aside for the reception of the corpses of the unburied dead. At intervals the road was strewn with cowries, while ghost-offerings such as pots, broken that their astral forms might be set free for the use of the shades, and lengths of cloth, faded by sun and rain, were to be seen in the bush on either hand. Here and there, too, a long, narrow crate formed of palm stems was passed, half covered by the dense undergrowth. In these the bodies of the unblest dead had been borne to their last resting-place, thence to be flung forth for vultures, ants and other carrion-feeding creatures to work their will upon—leaving but a handful of bleached bones for the luxuriant vegetation to cover with its charitable mantle.

Through these ill-omened shades we hurried, only stopping to pluck a new flower, the white cups of which together with masses of their strangely flattened calices had been found strewing the pathways of the beautiful Oban District, but hitherto it had been impossible to secure any leaves owing to the height of the trails, which had eluded discovery amid the network of giant branches to which they clung. Here, in the glade of the unburied dead, the path was festooned from side to side with spray upon spray, rich in flower, fruit and leaf.

Thence we crossed the market-place and, by a net-work of many mazy paths made apparently for no other purpose than to mislead chance-comers, reached an open space shaded by giant cotton trees and heavy-scented Monodoras. In the low bush round about sprang great aroids, said to be connected with the worship of the Thunder God's children. It is possible that the idea is due to the phallic-like appearance of the central spike, the long, thin, basal flowers of which give it somewhat the look of the Schlange im Schilf —the Pangwe description of the phallus.

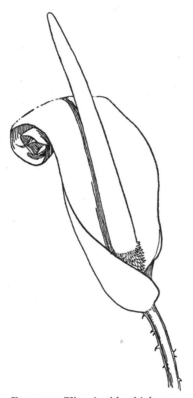

FIG. 21. The Aroid which grows round about the great Amad'onhia shrine at Ozozo

At the further end of the space lay the compound of the head priest, its open sheds full of cult objects but deserted; for the priest and all his family had fled at our approach.

Towards the near end of the cleared space two paths branched off, one on either side of a great clump of trees, the gnarled roots of which stretched right across as though barring the way. These two paths join later by a second group of no great size, which has sprung up round the riven base of a forest giant, the remains of whose trunk, lightning-scarred, may still be seen stretching far out into the bush beyond. Some few yards away a palm-leaf screen is placed across, shutting off the cleared space from the priest's compound. In the midst of the screen a little erection like the door-frame to a miniature house may be seen thickly plastered with the blood and feathers of sacrificed fowls. For about seven feet before this the ground is broken as though continually disturbed, and here and there in the soft sand depressions may be found as though round-bottomed water-jars had been set therein. This was explained as follows:

When pilgrims come hither bringing the appointed gifts, the priest first makes sacrifice and afterwards calls aloud the special favour which the worshipper has come to ask. Should Amad'ongha be favourably inclined, so soon as the prayer is finished, the roll of his thunder begins to sound, no matter how clear the sky. Then, with a great crash, a ball of stone about seven inches across falls from the blue overhead. This is the sign of the god himself, come down from his home in the clouds to bless the earth folk.

In vain we looked upwards, expecting to see branches which might serve to hide these mysterious missiles. Nothing was to be seen above but slender twigs tossing a delicate tracery of scarce open leaves against the blue.

On the far side of the fence, however, stretched part of the high priest's compound; so, if the means by which the seeming miracle was worked baffled discovery, the probable agency, at least, was not far to seek.

Later we learned that the name of the priest was Chioma Madume, and after some difficulty we succeeded in overcoming his dread of meeting a white man—a matter which had hitherto been considered as tabu. He was even persuaded to come with his two assistant priests to visit us. He proved to be a strange and somewhat pathetic figure, borne on a rude litter, thin, pale and with only one foot; the other, according to his own account, had 'rotted away and dropped off.' The skin of his two attendants was of that peculiarly vivid red occasionally met with in these regions. This appears to bear out Sir Harry Johnston's theory of an original red stock, but is explained by Ibo as showing that man or woman so marked out is a child of Amade Onhia. Both among the last named people and the Kalabari the law of the Thunder God ordains that all such shall be devoted to his service and become 'slaves of the Juju' unless ransomed by their family for a heavy sum. A sister of chief G. A. Yellow was thus chosen on account of the redness of her skin but was afterwards ransomed.

Chioma Madume gave the following account:

I myself have been priest of Amade Onhia for seven years.[1] Before me my father, Madume, held the office for

[1] No information could be obtained as to whether the priest 'died' at the end of the seventh year of his office, like the priest of the Aya-Eke cult at Elele, *vide* p. 103 *et seq.*

about the same time and before him my grandfather, Odu Kerin, ruled—I cannot tell for how long.

Our god is a very great god and is the only one throughout this region who gives a visible sign of his presence. When he wishes us to sacrifice or perform ceremonies for him, we ask a sign whereby we may know that this is really his will. In answer he sets a rainbow in the sky. When he descends into the shrine before the screen of plaited palm, the rainbow comes down also and hangs just above the place, thereby showing his presence. Many thunder stones fall there and the holes in the ground before the shrine are caused by something which falls from the sky, denting the earth; but it is invisible. No man has looked upon its shape.

(This assertion is in direct contradiction to the statements of pilgrims, who declared, as above related, that the holes were caused by stone balls, roughly speaking, seven inches in diameter, which fell down from above. It was, however, explained by one of the chiefs present that it was probably unlawful for the priest to describe the mysterious missiles—the outward, visible sign of the Thunder God's power.)

Chioma continued:

Amade Onhia, like Ale and the Aro Chuku Juju, is against all those who act contrary to native custom. The Thunder God sends down his bolt to strike such sinners; so, when a man is killed by lightning, people always know that he has done some bad thing. Witches and wizards specially dread his power and never dare to go out during a storm.

It was explained, in all seriousness, that the reason Amade Onhia so often sends his lightning to strike tall trees or hill tops is because he is jealous of all things which seek to raise themselves near to his kingdom. Only the birds may venture safely into the sky realm.

The children of earth should keep close to the breast of their mother. The idea seems contradictory to that held among some Etche Ibo and Aro as to the efficacy of sacrifices made to the so-called ' palms of the Thunder God ' mentioned on p. 46.

With Amafa Ibo this jealousy is thought to be developed along curious lines. Among this people it is forbidden for a woman to climb to any height, up a tree trunk or even over the top of a wall or fence. So strictly is the tabu enforced that ' civil war ' actually broke out among this people because the late chief Oosi, father of the present head chief of Amafa, built himself a ' story-house,' *i.e.* a two-floor building raised above the ground upon a foundation of piles—and allowed his women to go up and down the stairs. That this superstition obtains also among Isokpo Ibo is shown by a complaint brought before me by two men of Nkarahia as to the treatment accorded them by the chiefs of their town who were enraged because they had ventured to build themselves a ' story-house,' to the top rooms of which they allowed their women to climb. The chiefs declared that this endangered the safety of the town; for, should Amade Onhia hurl his bolt at the offending structure, peradventure he might punish the whole people for this disregard of his laws by two of their number.[1]

At sacred places, such as the shrine at Ozozo, the grove at Young Town or the sacred bush at Ngeri-Baw-Ama, no leaf may be picked nor branch broken.

[1] The tabu among Okoba and Ale Nsaw Ibo against climbing palm trees is probably due to the same idea.

FIG. 22. The shape, surrounded by skulls and draped with blood-stained
linen, which represents the earth goddess Ale in the shrine at Ewafe

To every one of the great Jujus slaves can run throughout the Ibo country and become its servants, after which no man has power to take them back without paying a great sum of money to the priest. In some cases even this is forbidden. In many parts of the interior such slaves can go into the market-place and take anything they want without payment; for no one dares touch them. After living for a long time with the Juju, they might sometimes go free; but could only go back to their native town at their own risk, for there their masters could recapture them. Amad'ongha and Ale have special power and their shrines are often placed near to one another, because this is pleasing to both, since they work together.

Perhaps the central part of Degama District may be looked upon as that where the worship of Ale holds chief sway. One of the strangest of her shrines lies at Ewawfe, in friendly nearness to church and school. Between them, more to the rear is a great, open shed, with elaborately fringed, corrugated iron roof. Beneath this are several clay pillars of the Ibudu type, before one of which some beautifully wrought torque-like bronze manillas lie amid a heap of smaller ones. A few yards off stands a small mud hut containing a figure of Ale indescribably gruesome with its strangely-shaped skull, its folds upon folds of blood-stained linen and the streams of blood poured and splashed over the supporting logs and the skulls and clumps of feathers thickly strewn around.

At this town it is customary to store all seed yams, etc., in the huts built for carrying out the rites of the ancestors—to whose care the germs of the new season's crops are thus entrusted.

Indeed, amongst many peoples here, the dead are thought to be more powerful even than Ale for the granting of fertility, especially as regards the crops, which is not surprising since they are supposed to live under the ground between incarnations on earth. In most parts, however, the fertility of the marriage bed, of the byre and of the crops is deemed to be chiefly due to the great Mother Goddess of the Earth. The duty is usually delegated to some of her subordinate tribes of Jujus and it is the members of one of these who are responsible for placing in the womb of the mother the spirit of the being about to be born on the earth plane. There is no ignorance here as to the necessary part played by the human father and mother, but their action would be fruitless and conception impossible without the help of the gods or jujus.

At the neighbouring village of Ogbokoro the chiefs were anxiously waiting to speak of a serious trouble which had befallen them. One of the schoolboys had broken the fence round the principal Ale shrine and stolen therefrom a quantity of manillas out of the mass of such which were to be seen, half smothered in feathers and congealed blood, upon the mud altar. On being assured that such desecration would be severely punished, the head chief answered:

This is a good word for us. We feel this thing very much. Ale is our mother and our god ; all that we have comes from her, and without her gifts we must indeed be lost.

As already mentioned, it is indicative of the reverence in which the Earth Goddess is held, that only the head chief of a town can aspire to be her priest. It is not without significance that the same rule holds with regard to the principal shrines of Amade Onhia. Only after pilgrimage to Ozozo may subsidiary lodges be erected, while the shrine of Ale is usually found nearby.

Where Amad'ongha is paramount, he appears to arrogate to himself the functions of Igwe, the Ibo sky god proper,[1] thus following in the footsteps of his Grecian prototype, 'Zeus, God of the bright sky,' who is also 'Zeus, God of the dark sky'; and it is in this capacity, as Lord of the drenching rain-storm, that he fertilises his consort the Earth Goddess.[2]

Of these mystic spousals of Earth and Sky perhaps the most beautiful picturing of all is to be found among the Ekoi of the South Cameroons and of Oban, Southern Nigeria.[3]

A curious link between the worship of Ale and the bearing of babes came to light one morning just as we were leaving Isokpo water-side, a market town of some importance on the banks of the upper New Calabar River. A long, shadeless march, by roads as yet practically unknown to white men, lay before us. We had risen at earliest dawn in order to place the first miles behind before the sun should add to the burdens of the carriers, when, just as we were setting forth after seeing the last load safely started, a complainant arrived with a letter appealingly held out in both hands. It was entitled 'To his Majesty the District

[1] Cf. p. 52.　　[2] *Zeus : A Study of Ancient Religion*, by A. B. Cook.
[3] Vide *In the Shadow of the Bush*, p. 14.

Commissioner. *Re* Wansumu *v.* Egeom. 17th February, 1915,' and ran as follows:

> Sir,
>
> I have the honour, most respectfully, to lodge this my humble complaint before your kind worship. . . .
>
> I am living in the defendant's town because it is my mother's city. Deceased is my brother. . . . His death took place in that month during which it is forbidden to die. By our native custom, should any one disobey this law, heavy expenses used to be paid before that person might be buried. Defendant knew that the place I am residing in is a mother city, yet he allowed me to perform all the ceremonies on behalf of the deceased Wawesi without assistance. . . .
>
> Leaving this for your discretion
>
> I have the honour to be,
>
> Sir,
>
> Your obedient servant,
>
> WANSUMU (his X mark).

On reading this document, it struck an ignorant white man as somewhat strange that there should be any month ' in which it is forbidden to die.' On this point the complainant stated:

> The man died in the seventh month of the year. Now according to our native law and custom no unmarried man may be buried during the seventh moon of the year. Should any die at that time, none may take notice of his passing and no relative may show sign that a death has taken place; for the seventh moon is the month of our mother Ale and by her law it is forbidden for anyone to die during this holy time. Most of all does she forbid the death of the unfruitful, whether man or woman. The bodies of such must be thrown away with all secrecy and may not be buried. The only exception to this rule is in the case of a man belonging

to a very rich family. Then, in consideration of the property
left, some of the relatives may undertake the expense necessary
for carrying out his funeral rites. Should a man die during
the holy month of Ale many purificatory ceremonies must be
gone through. This law extends over the whole of our
country lying round Isokpo part.

When questioned on the subject, chief G. Yellow
owned that a similar ' rule ' exists among Kalabari,
but is only enforced during the day on which an Owu
play is given. He added that the prohibition as to
burial applied also to those who die of certain diseases.
' When such people die,' he said,

a certain mark is visible upon the body. The flesh of such
an one looks decomposed, whereon people say ' Ale has
forsaken him!' Such bodies must be carried far from
the town and, if buried at all, it must be a long way from the
haunts of men. When a woman dies in childbirth, her
death is concealed for the same reason, since to pass away
before bearing a babe is displeasing to Ale. In such a case,
a corpse must be carried forth at night secretly through the
back door of the house. Young maids and pregnant women
may never see the body of one so accursed. By native law
all the property of the dead must be destroyed by fire, lest
the ban of sterility should pass to any who might afterwards
make use of such things.

Among Okrikans, during the seven days on which
the feast of the Earth Goddess, called by this tribe
Elechu, is held, a similar rule obtains. Should a
man die, he may not be buried but must be flung away
into the ' bad bush ' set apart for such outcasts. Only
if the family be rich enough to support the cost of the
purificatory ceremonies necessary before the goddess

can be appeased, may the dead be laid to rest in the breast of the Earth Mother—thence, like sown seed, to spring forth to new life.   The spirits of the accursed corpses flung into the place of ' bad bush ' on the other hand become Akalagoli or Ekwensu and on such the gate of reincarnation is closed for ever.   They haunt waste places and lonely creeks, seeking to harm those who still dwell in the sunshine.   Specially at noon or midnight is their evil power most to be dreaded.

Should pot or bowl be let fall, or wooden implement broken, during the feast of Elechu, the sherds must be piled in a heap upon which is flung the body of any animal which should die during the festival.   So large had these mounds grown in many cases that they formed a serious menace to the health of the town and proved no inconsiderable difficulty in the way of an official with leanings towards sanitation.   It is to a mixture of good fortune on the one hand and reasonableness on the part of the Okrikans that the trouble is now, for practical purposes, a matter of past history.

Among Ibibio the burial of women dying in childbirth is also forbidden.   These were borne forth, through a hole purposely broken in the house wall, to be flung away in the bush, lest their barrenness might have ill effect upon the fruitfulness of the Earth Mother.

VI

IBUDU

To those who pass through the country with open eyes it is obvious that the phallic cult is very strong among Ibo. Where the Ibibio had contented themselves with a plain mud pillar, set as emblem amid the farm, Ibo take special pains in modelling not only a personification of the symbol, but in showing unmistakably that the circumcised phallus is intended to be represented.

Among Ibo, as with the ancient Egyptians also, the feminine, as well as the male, genital organs are worshipped. Both are rudely depicted under the title Ibudu—a name which embraces the chief protective Jujus [1] erected in town or compound, the primary purpose of which appears to be the granting of piccans, though most also act as protector in general to the family or village of which they are the fetish, and bestow fertility on farm and byre. The feminine part of the Juju is usually in bell shape, instead of the pot or calabash form found among Ekoi and Ibibio. It generally shows the high coiffure only permitted to Ibo women after the birth of a babe. The nose is often joined to the base of the hair ridge and the

[1] Many of these would now be classified by me as symbols of 'medicines' or charms, not 'jujus.' Vide *The Peoples of Southern Nigeria*, vol. ii. p. 153.

impaled tortoise, already explained as a feminine symbol, is as a rule seen in the foreground.

Perhaps the most convincing testimony to the efficacy attributed to the feminine genital organ is a carefully carved representation of the labia, which was explained as having been one of the most sacred objects in a great Andoni Juju house, whence it was taken by a man who had no idea of its significance. In course of time it came to my notice and was subsequently added to our collection.

An example of the simplest form of phallic pillar may be found in a compound next door to that of Ababua, head chief of Omo Chuku. Save for two roughly modelled feet at the base, no attempt was made to add limbs to the column, down either side of which a row of rough wooden pegs had been driven. It was explained that each man of the compound inserted one of these on taking a wife, so that the Juju might have a constant reminder of the need to send ' plenty of piccans ' to their hearth.

In another quarter of the same town, in front of Omo Alipo compound, an Ibudu may be seen of which the pillar represents a body from the loins upward— the hands, so roughly modelled as more nearly to resemble feet, resting upon the circular base as though in the act of lifting the upper part through from the earth beneath. The figure is headless; only the end of the central pole and the twigs and tie-tie forming the core, round which such images are modelled, protrude from the broken rim. It is perhaps worth remarking that this pillar, like some to be mentioned later,

FIG. 23. Obelli Oduaha Ibudu juju for granting many piccans

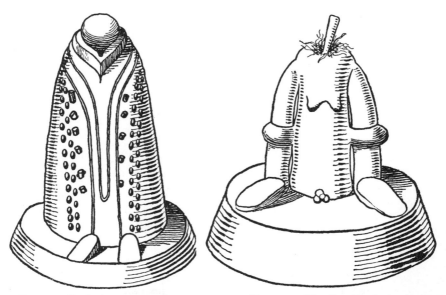

FIG. 24. Ibudu in compound next
to Chief Ababua's, Omo Chuku

FIG. 25. Headless Ibudu in Omo
Alipo compound, Omo Chuku

combines both male and female attributes, somewhat
in the style of the Indian Linga.

Perhaps the most highly conventionalised of all such
images is one to be found in a shrine built in a pro-
minent position on the main road, just outside the
Omo-Ofo quarter of Ndelle. This represents the
male part of the Juju. At the other end of the shed
a smaller figure is to be seen, bell-shaped and showing
feminine symbols. This is typical of most of those
intended to represent the feminine creative power,
though one of a type more nearly approaching the male
form of Ibudu was found, later on, in Chief Wokogg's
compound at Omo Akani, Owerri District.

Just beyond the shed containing the two phallic
pillars, a couple of shrines may be seen, one on either
side of the main road. That on the right is built in
honour of the Juju Onru-Ji (farm yam). This was
explained as ' one very big woman spirit, all same Ala.'
In the ground were many knives and pieces of iron,
said to have been placed there by order of the priest
who declared that the Juju needed them.

A little further, on the opposite side of the road
beneath an arbour-like cutting made in the thick bush,
was a piece of white baft stretched between two posts.
This is set up in honour of Onru Ka'n Ala, stated to
be the husband of Onru-Ji. The chief of the quarter
explained:

> Both of these Jujus are strong too much. Therefore we
> never swear a man on their name, because, should he even
> hesitate to tell the truth when brought before them, the
> spirit of one or other would strike him dead at once, giving

Fig. 26.   Ibudu at Ogaminni, near Ndelle

no time for repentance ! It is a very strong rule for our part that both Jujus must be dressed by the people of Omo-Ofo before they may eat new yams.

Fig. 27. Ite Uru Ibudu
See page 71

At Aloa, a town in the centre of the Division, a shrine is to be seen containing a fetish, the like of which is not, to the best of my belief, to be found elsewhere in these parts. It is in the corner of a room set apart as sacred to Chineke, the Creatrix, in the compound of Chief Wegu, and consists of an oblong block, terminating in a carefully modelled representation of the male genital organs, raised upon three steps. To this the owner makes sacrifice every month, usually at the time of the new moon, in order that ' plenty piccans ' may be born to those of his house.

A somewhat similar fetish was found among the Ale Nsaw Ibo in the shrine of Chief Idu of Oborotta

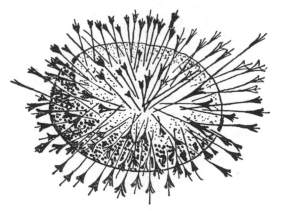

FIG. 28. Charm
*See page 7*1

raised upon a clay step in the angle of the wall at the right hand corner. This consisted of two small round pots fixed neck-downward into the clay, while between them protruded a piece of wood, roughly phallic in form, on the upper surface of which two miniature Offor sticks were bound lengthwise and side by side. The object of this fetish was to bring prosperity in general and, in particular, many children to the compound.

A Juju, intended to represent a woman's body from the waist downward, was found among the same people. This was called Ite Uru, *i.e.* pot of gain, and was supported at the rear by the wall and in front upon two roughly modelled legs. It formed the principal cult object in the shrine of Chief Okuroji of Obokoffia and was set up by the grandfather of the present head of the house, but had been freshly decorated (Fig. 27).

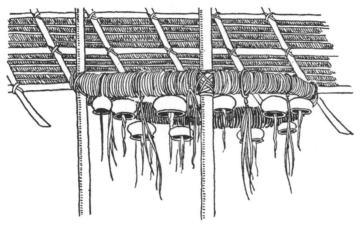

FIG. 29. Ibudu Nwa

Another Juju for bringing 'plenty piccans' to the house and for making them grow up fine, strong and tall—also for giving long life to its owner—was hung up to the roof over the main door of the head chief's house at Ndelle (Fig. 28). The arrows were planted so thickly that one could not see of what the oval groundwork was made.

At Ale-Barada, a charming town to the west of the Upper New Calabar River, never before visited by a white man, and which, as its name denotes, is under the special protection of the Earth Goddess, a Juju is to be found, called Ibudu Nwa, *i.e.* Ibudu for children. This occupies the centre of a rectangular shrine and is set beneath a canopy of tie-tie, attached to the roof, from which depend inverted pots, the shape of a shallow bell, each with a twist of gay-coloured cloth swinging, clapper-wise, from its centre. Beneath these hang fringes of palm-leaf, so long, in places, as almost to sweep the market-basket placed upon the neck of the strange, headless figure beneath (Fig. 29).

On marriage, before going to the bridegroom's house, each maiden of the town is brought by her friends to this shrine and, bending before the image, dips her hand into an earthen pot filled with 'medicine' which is placed there in readiness. Then she rubs her hands over the Juju, after which she laves them in a small bowl filled with pure water. Again she passes her left fingers over the image and afterwards over her own body; ' for ' as the head chief explained, ' Ibudu Nwa is a very strong Juju in our town and will surely grant fruitfulness to all those who carry out these rites. So we were taught by our forefathers and this we believe even to-day. Should any man doubt, he has but to look round and see the many piccans which are born to our town.'

Between the upraised arms, resting upon the place where the head should be, is a market basket, full of dried roots, seed yams, etc. Outside the shrine, each protected by a small shed, were two unusually large phallic pillars, to which bridegrooms bring offerings.

Across all, from post to post, rising like Venetian masts, were long chains made from linked rings of creeper, from which hung, at intervals, inverted bowls with gay-coloured strips of cloth waving to and fro in the

FIG. 30. Ibudu Nwa at Ale-Barada

breeze, like those decorating the canopy of Ibudu Nwa. To the left stood a great tree, its trunk hung round with white cloth, the reputed home of a powerful and beneficent nature spirit. Before the principal shrine sprang little saplings of the bush which Ale first brought when she came swimming through the wide waste of waters to form the first abiding place for her children—men, beasts, trees and flowers.

Altogether Ale-Barada is a charming spot and the manners of the sons of the soil were unusually gentle and friendly. They willingly answered every question, in striking contrast to the inhabitants of the next town, Oduaha, where a Juju of somewhat different type is to be found. This was sullenly explained to us as without name and only used for protection— ' not to give piccans.' The canoe upon its head was likewise stated to have been put there ' only to look fine. Not for any purpose.'

At Omo Hume, a quarter of Omo Dioga, another Ibudu was found, which was said to be intended as a representation of the Earth Goddess, here called Aja. In a little clearing to the right of the main road stood a shrine of unusual size, sheltering two phallic pillars. The smaller of these, placed in front and a little to the left, was obviously female and smeared with blood from the breast downward. The rear figure bore no name save ' Husband of Aja,' or at least none other was confided to us. So tall was this that it filled the whole space from floor to roof, looming, colossal and with a certain impressiveness, from out the shadows at the back of the shrine. Between the two, on either side, lay a piece of plaited palm-cloth, black and white, such as widows wear in some parts ; while two deep fringes of palm-leaf were hung before the entrance, screening the strange, rude deities within from the glances of passers-by.

It was explained that the cloths were those of barren women, and had been laid at the feet of Aja and her spouse in the hope that, when resumed by their owners, the ban of sterility, imposed through the hate of some rival, might be broken by the power of the fertility-bestowing Earth Gods.

At Bush Digiriga again, a small town to the east of the Sombreiro River inhabited by Abuan people and never before visited by Europeans—a Juju 'for the obtaining of piccans' is to be found, which in many ways resembles the Ibo Ibudu. About this particular fetish, however, there are certain points which we never met elsewhere. In addition to the high coiffure — a recognised

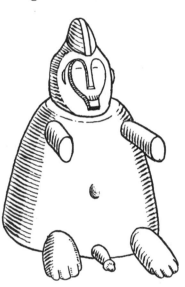

FIG. 31. Ibudu at Digiriga

symbol of femininity—the head is provided with a square beard in shape like those false ones worn during certain dynasties by Egyptian rulers, especially queens reigning in their own right. It is perhaps worth noting that, while the arms of the figure are mere stumps, without any attempt to reproduce hands, and the feet are so rude as to be almost shapeless, the phallus is modelled with the utmost care, showing that in the minds of its makers this detail was of very special significance.

Outside the entrance to the Omo Dara quarter of Akpani, an Ibudu of unique type may be seen, one looking-glass eye twinkling in the middle of its head beneath a ring of feathers set crown-wise in the clay. Before it, to a four-branched post, a medicine-pot was bound.

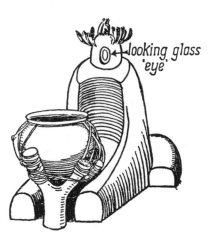

In the midst of the quarter, beneath a little palm-leaf hut, stands a group of Ibudu. The largest of the pillars represents the female, the smaller the male, attributes. They are modelled seated back to back—a prostrate leopard lying to the left and a crater-like mound, containing a pot for Juju medicine, to the right. Chief Woke Abara, head of the quarter, gave the following explanation:

Fig. 32. Ibudu placed before the entrance to Omu Dara quarter of Akpani

' Formerly it was very hard for us to get children. Nearly all our women were barren, so we raised the two Ibudu, one male and the other female. Since then we got plenty piccans in our town.' He added that the ' leopard spirit ' helps the Juju to prevent the deaths of children. The small cone in the foreground and the headless animal lying in front of this were the work of the few children then existing.

With regard to the figure of a leopard, it is perhaps worth remarking that the ancient kings of Benin were wedded, in mystic spousals, with a leopard bride. Also, among thòse Ibo dwelling in the group of towns round Igrita, the spirits of the righteous dead often take

FIG. 33. Ibudu at Akpani

up their abode in leopard form while awaiting a new term of earth life, but those who enter into crocodile, ape, or bush cat, are regarded as for ever accursed.

Amid a branch of Kalabari settled at Oguta in Owerri District, a type of Ibudu is to be found, not, so far as our knowledge goes, to be met with in other parts. Each of these emblems consists of two sphinx-like figures, one male and the other female, facing different ways but joined together by a ridge of clay, which forms, as it were, the back of the sphinx.

At the Ibo town on the far side of the beautiful Oguta lake, we came across another phallic pillar combining the figures of the dual personality, male and female, of the Ibudu Ezum Mezum. As in the case of the Ale shrine, described on page 74, the consort was nameless, bearing no designation save that of husband of Ezum Mezum. The figure representing him held the place of honour at the base of the column which symbolises the joint attributes of the Juju; while, at a height almost double that of the husband, towers the face of the wife. On either side of the pillar, out-topping the male figure from the neck upwards, climb two great crocodiles; while placed here and there, at irregular intervals, human heads stand out in high relief.

Chief Onomonu, the owner of the shrine, told us:

> The Ibudu Ezum Mezum is mostly worshipped at Amaii in Abaw District and priests came thence to build this shrine for us. It was made at a time when a great sickness was raging in our town, in the hope of staying this scourge, granting protection and prosperity in general and especially to help our people in the bearing of piccans.

At its installation, about twelve years ago, the Abaw doctors held a great ' smelling out,' and, in consequence, decreed that the epidemic was caused by the witchcraft of the six *richest* women of the town, who must therefore be put to death and their property be made over to the medicine men! When informed of their doom, the victims refused to acquiesce and were therefore beaten to death in the market-place. The number of heads, modelled at irregular intervals over the pillar, corresponds to that of the victims thus slaughtered at the inauguration ceremonies—four at the back and two in front, between the sacred crocodiles. All are liberally smeared with blood poured upon the heads and trickling downward. This is the only example known to us at the time in which an Ibudu is so represented as to show the dual creative forces, male and female, combined so as to form a single pillar. Many Ibudu were later seen among the Abaw Ibo of Kwale District, where this particular type of symbol would seem to have reached its greatest development.

The phallic figures, above mentioned, are, however, by no means the only examples met with in West Africa of the mingling, in one object, of male and female symbols. For instance, the emblem of the greatest of all Ekoi Jujus, Eja, unmistakably combines the two. Here, the phallus, represented with the uttermost pains and fidelity, is the sign of the harvest god himself, while the bowl-like object to which it is attached represents the womb of his wife Ekumoke. The united symbol stands upon a base formed of wide-open human jaws.[1]

Among the Ekoi, both in the South Cameroons and Southern Nigeria, as indeed throughout the greater part of the West Coast generally, a pot or calabash is regarded as a feminine symbol, and it is of considerable significance that traces of male semen have been found

[1] *In the Shadow of the Bush*, p. 76.

in no inconsiderable number of the pots set before
Ibudu images and in other Juju shrines throughout
the Ibo country. This fact is vouched for by a
medical officer.

In the ritual chant sung by Ekoi at the festival of
Eja, which is also the feast of the first fruits, the names
of the combined deities are always invoked :

> Man Eja!   I am staying with you.
> O, I am staying with you!
> Ekumoke !   I am staying with you.
> O, I am staying with you !

Of these two deities it was expressly stated: ' Eja
is male and the most strong.   Ekumoke is less strong
than Eja; nevertheless without her help he can do
nothing.'

During the annual rites a woman was formerly
sacrificed and the genital organs cut out and laid in
the sacred pot, which contains the ' medicine ' of the
cult.   Since the coming of Government it has naturally become increasingly difficult to obtain this
necessary ingredient, and it was a matter of grave
anxiety on the part of the priest lest the power of the
Juju should decrease in consequence.

Amidst some of the eastern Ibo sub-tribes and the
northern Semi-Bantu, the ancestors are represented by
small clay pillars or mounds, clay balls or round or
pointed stones, before which sacrifices are made and
prayers offered for the granting of fertility, especially
at the two great festivals of the year, the planting of
farms and the harvest.

In those parts of the country where rock is available, *i.e.* among the northern Yoruba and Semi-Bantu, many stone monoliths may be found, some of which are unmistakably phallic, while others are used not only for this worship but also as ancestral memorials. In fact, the two cults are inexplicably mixed, as is natural when it is remembered that amongst these peoples fruitfulness is, to a large extent, attributed to the forefathers. Some of these memorials date back many hundreds of years; a fuller description will be found in Chapter XVII, vol. ii, of *The Peoples of Southern Nigeria*.

In the club-houses of the great Ekkpe secret society the sacrifices are made before a phallic monolith, which represents the former members of the club as also the tutelary deity, while in, or near, its base are generally placed rounded pebbles, the symbol of the Earth Goddess. A similar monolith is worshipped amongst many of the Bantu and Bafumbum-Bansaw as a representation of the supreme deity.

VII

EKU

ALL over the western part of the District a strange rite still obtains which is obviously only another manifestation of the phallic cult. As there are local differences it will be necessary to describe separately the peculiarities of each centre.

By the roadside near Umo Abale, a quarter of Omo Dioga, half hidden amid grass and creepers, we came across a crowd of figures formed of sun-baked clay, cone-shaped and painted black. Further on, in front of almost each compound, smaller groups were to be seen, usually arranged at the base of some Juju tree, or round a sapling of the sacred Ogrisi (*Dolichandrone* sp.). In several cases circular moulds of baked clay, much like an old-fashioned spittoon in shape, lay nearby. It was explained that upon these the girls of each compound, after undergoing the initiatory ceremonies preparatory to marriage, set the food cooked as an offering to the Eku, as the phallic figures are called. This word is also used to designate the cones of baked clay used to support cooking-pots. Should any girl, after arriving at the age of puberty and being inducted into the feminine mysteries, neglect to set up such an image each year, about the time of making new farms, until she becomes a member of her husband's house, no babes would bless their

FIG. 34. Eku at Umo Abale quarter of Omo Dioga

union. In one or two cases a slight amount of decoration, formed by lines drawn with the fingers in the soft clay, has been added; while here and there an attempt was made to surmount the cone by what was explained as a representation of the high head-dress only allowed to Ibo women after the birth of a babe. Mostly, however, the images showed nothing more or less than a simple attempt at depicting the phallus.

About a month later, at the house of Chief Ugwa in the Oturu quarter of Akpani, Eku of a still simpler type were found, together with clay pot-rests of much the same shape as those already described; while just outside, in the bush by the roadside, we came upon some thirty or more phallic figures, the tallest and frankest yet seen. Some stood on circular, some on rectangular, bases; but on each the membrum virile was modelled with especial care.

It was explained that every year, when making the more elaborate pillars, each betrothed girl fashions several of the plainer type, a foot to a foot and a half in height. These are said to be used as ' strong Juju on which to swear people.' [1] Three of these are borne by each maid to her bridegroom's compound, there to be presented to the chief woman of the family, by whom they are set together to support the pot in which food is cooked for the future husband. When ready, this is poured into a native bowl and placed upon the clay ring. After marriage, the bride comes to the new home and herself cooks her husband's

[1] It is perhaps worth remarking that among Mbolli all fire brick is used for the same purpose.

meals upon the same three pillars prepared by her own hands.

It is not without significance that the trinity of cone-shaped pillars, with cup-like depressions, raised before the Kalabari Nduen Fobara (ancestral shrines), into which libations to the forefathers are poured every eighth day, are of almost identical type. At Oru-Sangama, an ancient town on a creek leading into the San Bartholomeo River, we came across two of these small cones modelled within a circle, also of clay, beneath the palm-leaf roof of a tiny hut. So like were these to the Eku emblems that we took for granted that the little shrine was but another dwelling-place of one of the manifold representations of Ibudu Omu-mu, *i.e.* the Ibudu of fertility. Long sojourn in Africa should, however, teach caution even to the most careless enquirer, and we therefore, as always, took the precaution to keep our ideas to ourselves and asked the significance of the symbol. As a result we were told that they represented the Nduen Fobara of a neighbouring house. Our informant added:

> Some men make three, some two, small pillars for the pouring out of libations to the spirits of their dead. Some again make only one such emblem for the reception of drink offerings. Here no carved images are shown as is usual in rich Kalabari towns; the cones themselves represent the ancestors, except in the case of men of distinction.

Considering the peculiar powers thought by many tribes to attach to the phalli of the dead, especially those of warriors or others who excelled in strength or power, as also the Egyptian legend of the birth of

FIG. 35. Pillars, carved tusks, and bronze torques. Kalabari Shrine of Awome-Ka-So

Horus—that seed of life, snatched by the widowed Isis from Death himself—it is perhaps not too far fetched an idea to imagine that the likeness of symbol was intended to signify a connection between the physical body of the new-born and the astral shape or ethereal mould, supplied in most cases according to general belief from the ghost realm, where the ancestral shades await reincarnation—by preference in the bodies of those about to be born to the family to which they themselves formerly belonged.

Sir James Frazer, in his wonderful *Golden Bough*, tells of sacrificial victims whose phalli were beaten with twigs—not out of cruelty, but with the idea of increasing the powers of virility. Among the Ekkett Ibibio sacred boughs are drawn over the pudenda of warriors while parts are even cut off and buried secretly by the marriage bed, in the byre or on the farm. In this connection it is perhaps worth mentioning that one of the most dreaded of West African tortures, employed upon captives of distinction, was the continued flagellation of the phalli.

Chief Igo, of Omo Nelu, gave the following information:

We start to make the Eki—as they are locally called—at the time of cutting the undergrowth for the new farms. Then, when we have carried out the images and set them up by the roadside, we begin clearing away the top branches. The ornamented pot-rests are used for cooking chop for the Eki.

Chief Chuku's quarter cooks for two weeks (*i.e.* sixteen days). Amadi's and my quarter cook for thirty days. It is the young girls who make these things—both the cooking ones and the others. For twenty-five days we hold the first

festival, that of the low round Eki, which we call Eki Mother.
Every evening at about five o'clock time the girls cook. On
the twenty-fifth day each girl starts making one of the high
Eki, Ada Eki (eldest daughter of Eki), which is worshipped
for five days before carrying it out. When my father was
alive, the ceremony always started in his compound; for he was

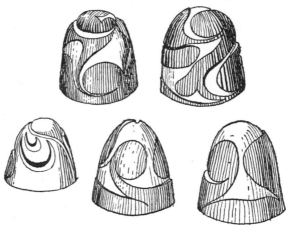

FIG. 36. Patterns of the low Eki

the head chief. After he had made festival for eight days,
all the other compounds joined in and continued till thirty
days were finished. Then all men took notice and said: ' It
is now time to start the new farms.'

With us also the young girls go and get ant-hill earth
before they make the Eki, but they do not use it for these,
only keep it in their houses for three months and afterwards
take it with them to the market-place, where they dance
and play round it and then finally throw it away.

Egu 'Nde 'Nwayin is a woman's festival held at the time
of digging new yams. It was my father, the priest of Ale,
who set the time for this ceremony also. At this time the
women dress very finely, wearing many beads round their
ankles.

On another occasion, just after leaving Ndelle en route for Rumoji, we found, by the side of a bush path beneath the spreading branches of a Berlinia, a hut, the long, low, palm-leaf roof of which was covered with the fragrant white-petalled flowers showered down from above. Under this shelter was a platform of clay some twenty feet in length, carefully smoothed and with gaily coloured plates set at intervals along its edge. Upon this a double row of strangely-shaped finely-decorated figures were to be seen, formed of sun-dried clay, much in the style of the Eku already mentioned, but far more elaborately modelled and painted. On the bright yellow clay, ridges and lines of shining black, vivid blue and white were to be seen, while each was surmounted with an attempt to represent the elaborate styles of coiffure affected by girls of marriageable age.

Each had been brought thither by a maiden of the neighbourhood after undergoing initiatory rites in company with her ' age class.' The ceremonies are conducted in places set apart, under the leadership of elderly women of the town. The time chosen is after the planting of new farms when the seeds first germinate. At this season all little maids who have reached, or are approaching, the age of puberty—for the ' age class ' includes those born within three years of one another—come together to be instructed, by matrons chosen for the purpose, in all that it is thought necessary for them to know as a preparation for marriage. Later, the neophytes return to their parents' house and there model the figures shown in the photograph. When all are ready they go, together with their instructress and a band of relatives, each bearing one of the Eku upon her head in procession to the spot chosen by priest or instructress. Here a platform of clay, decorated with insets of plates, pieces of looking-glass, etc., has already been prepared. The celebrants in turn place thereon the queerly shaped image which is supposed to be necessary in order to draw down upon the girl, who offers it, the blessing of fertility.

Beside those newly initiated, older maidens, to whom the mysteries have formerly been revealed but who are as yet unwedded, also take part in the rite, bearing a fresh Eku in the procession, year after year until the whole, or at any rate the main part, of the dowry has been paid, and they leave their parents' house for that of a husband. The elder girls offer images often over a yard in height, while the new initiates bring smaller ones, proportionate to their size.

At a little distance from the places set apart for the principal images, fish racks may occasionally be seen by the roadside and on, or between them, the smallest figures of all are to be found. These are said to represent ' the slaves of the Eku.' Each girl, after modelling her own symbol, makes at least one such little attendant, so that her image may be well served.

Near Ndelle waterside a somewhat different arrangement obtains. In front of the long line of Eku, a separate group may usually be found set round a sapling of the sacred Ogrisi tree. The central figure is dedicated to the principal girl of the town, while

FIG. 37. Group of Eku, near 'Ndelle

the smaller ones grouped round her represent her attendants. Near the centre, springing out of the clay base, was a small sprig of the bush which Ale brought with her when she first formed the earth.

At the same time of year, when the seed corn and yams lie awaiting rebirth in the womb of the Earth Mother, the unmarried girls of Elele carry out a ritual similar in many respects but with certain points of difference. Here the images are modelled from clay supplied not by the parents, as is usual in other parts, but by the bridegroom. These must be rubbed and smoothed for seven days and each is surmounted by a head, the coiffure of which is carefully copied from that of the girl herself. Every evening, food offerings are carried to the place where the Eki are set up, while the girls dance and sing before them. The bridegroom must provide from sixty to a hundred Awarawu manillas during this time, which are accepted by the parents as part of the dowry.

Often these strange images are modelled with breasts in addition to the male emblem. Is it an unwarrantable assumption to think that this may possibly be intended as a primitive attempt at picturing the ideal marriage, in which male and female attributes play equal parts ? This peculiarity is not confined to the Eku but is even more marked in many Ibudu, as for instance the one already mentioned at the Umo Alipo compound, Omo Chuku.[1]

Some time after all the Eki have been set up in the farms, compounds and bush round Elele, preparations

[1] See p. 66.

are made for the carrying out of a further ceremony,
called Nwan Aja, *i.e.* Child of the Earth, which is said
to be closely related to the festival already described.
For this, the unmarried girls of Elele go out to the
bush and search round until each has found one of
the great mounds thrown up by termites. ' With the
help of relatives she digs down into this until she
comes to the heart of the cave, named in our speech

FIG. 38. The Wekwe Eruru

Wekwe Eruru.' The floor of this looks like a moun-
tain range in miniature. Breathless with excitement,
the little maid counts the number of peaks; for just
as many as there are of these, so many babes she will
bear. With infinite pains, that not one may be broken
off, she cuts round, then lifts the flat, roughly circular
mass to her head and carries it home. This is a time
of great anxiety; for, should any part break away
during the process, the number of fallen points denotes
—alas!—the still-born babes which fate will send
her.

In some places all the girls of the quarter join together
to seek out an ant hill and dig up the part in which

dwells the queen ant. ' One of their number is appointed to carry this thing, which is then borne back to the town and set down on the road near some of the principal compounds. All stand watching to see in what direction the ants will go; for the way they take points out the compound in which the girls are to live until the time of the new yam harvest. There they must stay in seclusion, grinding cam wood and preparing for the approaching festival. Thither their future husbands come bringing palm-wine, yams and fish, together with six Awarawu manillas as dash for the owner of the compound.'

From many indications we had long suspected that the magic powers of the ant hill proceeded, in part at least, from its phallic resemblance. This was borne out by the number of Ibudu shrines, avowedly raised for the increase of children, before which these curious structures, known in these parts as ' Bush-men,' were found. In several, one of these lesser ant hills had been set up amid the special ' servants of the Juju ' modelled on either hand of the principal image. Such an one is to be seen in the shrine of Ezum Mezum, erected within the compound of the Aro chief Ogunda of Azu-Miri near Nkarahia. On each side of the pillar stand her ' servants.' The nearest, a conventionalised phallic pillar surmounted by a head and with a little doorway in its tower-like base, through which one of the small elongated chalk cones—offered by every woman of the compound after conception—is seen, half in and half out, so as to appear in the act of entering. Next to this, but further from the image, is a natural ant hill, daubed with paint, against which leaned several of the lesser symbols.

These chalk cones or images, though more roughly moulded, bear considerable resemblance to those carefully modelled in clay and suspended over their father's shrine by each ' true daughter ' of an Ibibio chief in the Mkpokk region to show that they were the

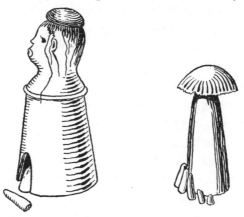

FIG. 39. The ' Servants of Ezum-Mezum '

legitimate offspring of the dead man, not of slaves, or of ' widows ' born to the house, of whom he was only titular parent.

At the end of their period of seclusion in Nwan Aja's compound, the girls of Elele put on new cloths and gay ornaments, then sally forth to market (Eke Oma). This is a sign that the play is ended for the time.

Every other year a special play is given. According to Mr. D. Braid: ' This cannot be carried out more often, on account of the great expense incurred therein by the bridegroom. The name of this play is Ajiji '—

in some places Adidi or Adadi—' and it is one of the best of all plays for girls and ladies. It looks grand whenever they start same. They dress with brass ornaments, corals, etc., on their feet, all which expenses are run by the husbands, with the exception of the anklets for one foot which the parents are expected to provide. The brass ornaments are prepared by the blacksmiths, from nine Awarawu manillas for growing up ladies and four to five for younger girls. All go in procession round the town until they come to a place in the Omuneta quarter called Ebu, where there is a great tree in which dwells a certain powerful Juju. Here fowls are sacrificed and cut in such a manner that blood falls upon the feet of each girl. After this has been done, they sing all kinds of songs, dancing with great gladness for some hours.'

Both on the way there and back those girls who are about to marry rich men are carried in decorated chairs, with a canopy

fastened above them. Bearers are hired for this service by the future husbands. During the Ajiji ceremony many ghosts flock into the town. In olden days, these would strike the girls as they were borne by; because spirits are jealous of any mortal whose feet are not set upon the ground. A bride thus struck always sickens and usually dies within the year. That is the reason why, nowadays, each girl holds a picture before her, so that the ghosts may strike at this and let her go by unharmed.

On reaching home a feast is given by the parents and next morning all the girls take chop to the husbands' place. This food is distributed to all in his compound, together with rewards of money. The bridegroom is expected to do the same in return and all the expenses incurred by him at this time are counted as dowry. The play generally lasts for seven Ekes, *i.e.* about two months.

In October 1916, just outside Elele, on the Nkarahia road, a group of specially interesting symbolic images was found. It consisted in roughly modelled male and female figures, arranged in pairs and lying out-stretched at the base of a great cotton tree (Akpu). The bays, formed by its buttress-like roots, were separated from one another by giant snakes moulded in clay, which, arranged in irregular loops, usually with the tail of one against the tail of the other, served to fence off the sacred enclosure from the wayside. Within the various bays thus formed smaller serpents twined and twisted, often placed between the male and female figures. In one case the phallic serpent was shown in the act of entering the body of a woman.

Dotted over the slope, forked sticks were seen driven into the ground or raised on little clay mounds. From these depended strings of great snail shells (*Acatina marginata*) or empty fish racks, in shape much like the head of a Badminton racquet.

This group, the name of which was given as Akpu Ogbe Ajiji, had been modelled by maidens of marriage-able age belonging to Chief Woyike's compound as an additional means of increasing fertility.

Just beyond Elele Aliminni, on the Ndelle road, a great tree may be found to the Genius of which the unmarried girls of the neighbourhood go and pray during the Ajiji—locally called Adidi—ceremony. Three circular clay steps are built, one above the

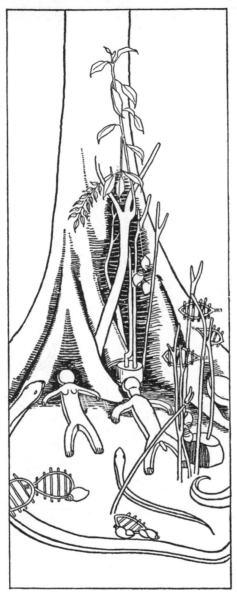

Fig. 40. Clay figures at base of cotton tree near Elele

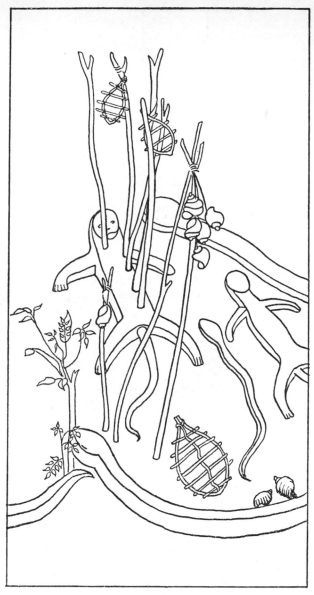

Fig. 41. Figures at base of cotton tree near Elele

See p. 94

other, round the base of the tree and reaching about
four feet up its trunk, forming a rough altar upon which
piles of *Acatina marginata* shells and empty fish racks
(Paka Eji) were laid.   A few yards further, in front of
the compound of Chief Ofonda, a large terminal bud
of the banana flower-spike, pierced with four slivers of
wood was set up on a tall palm stalk.   This bud is
called Eni Awsoku, *i.e.* navel of plantain or banana.
It is natural enough that these two trees should bear

Fig. 42. The Eni Awsoku

special significance in the fertility rites.   The combination of phallic-shaped fruit and terminal bud with its
oval form offers an obvious symbol of the male and
female reproductive organs.

    After building the Adidi altar and setting up Eni
Awsoku, the celebrants go in procession round the
town, their faces rubbed with chalk of a pale café au
lait shade and their hair covered with bright yellow
paste.   From a distance this colouring gives them a
curiously European look.   At the back, hanging
round the waist, they wear a kind of apron of large glass
beads, arranged in alternate squares, usually green and
brown in colour, the whole fringed with little brass balls.

After a girl has been given in marriage and has gone to live with her husband, she may never again take part in the Ajiji play. At the end of the series of Eku ceremonies, which last, roughly speaking, from the ending of farm planting to harvest time, the whole town of Elele goes to Chief Eleche's compound for the feast of new yams which is held in honour of the great Juju Aya-Eke. On this occasion every man, woman and child bears a gift to the priest. Even little babes, too small to stand alone, are borne before him. The mothers press a gift into the tiny hands and then hold them out towards the chief that not even the smallest should fail to make offering.

The name Ajiji, given by Ibo to the greatest play in the series, would seem to be derived from Aja (sacrifice), which is also in some parts the name of the Earth Goddess herself, and Ji (yam).

VIII

THE YAM CULT

At the cutting of new farms most Ibo chiefs make sacrifice to Ale and again before harvest. Beside offerings to her, some should also be made to the Ajokko-Ji[1] or Njokkoji—the king (or Juju) yam, the biggest one of all the crop in which the yam spirit is thought to take up its abode. This is always set aside from one season to another, and when bird or beast is slain in sacrifice to the Genius of the farm, the blood is thrown upon the Ajokko-Ji.

Should a man find that he has more yams one year than in the seasons before, he brings the richest sacrifice in his power and offers it in thanks to the Farm Spirit for giving increase and doing good to him. The word Ajokko means Juju, but it is also used with the signification of 'great' and 'mighty.' This king yam, as it is sometimes called, is kept throughout the whole year until next harvest comes round. Either fowls' or goats' blood should be poured out in libation upon it. Formerly a spirit dwelt within, which protected all the yam racks in the farm. Now, owing to the dying out of such beliefs, people are not afraid to steal from these. In olden days they never dared to do such a thing for dread of the yam Juju.

While visiting Oppe, a farm settlement just outside Alessa, we were shown a 'strong Juju' connected

[1] The Ajokko-Ji, the Yam Spirit, is further described in *The Peoples of Southern Nigeria*.

with the worship of Nkike, the Mbolli Earth Goddess.
This was formed from a collection of skulls, yams and
other roots, bound round with tie-tie into the form
of a gigantic yam and then attached to a stout stake,
the end of which was sharply pointed for driving into
the ground.   This symbol was said to take, for the

Fig. 43.   Ife Ja Okko or Ife Ajokko at Ogu

Mbolli, the place of the giant Ajokko-Ji to which Ibo
offer sacrifice.

A more elaborate substitute was found at Ogu on the
Niger—a town occupied by a sub-tribe of Ibo, allied
to those of Onitsha.   There, in the house of one of the
secondary chiefs, a row of small pots was seen, set in
the clay floor, along one side of the verandah.   These
were explained as the Ife Ajokko—called Ife Ja-Okko
by some—which for this tribe take the place of the
Ajokko-Ji.   There were nine pots of different shape;
the number was explained by saying that, as each chief
succeeded to the headship of the house, a new Ife

Ajokko was made. Eight, therefore, were those belonging to the ancestors.

Among Mbolli the phallic pillars are of a peculiar type mostly carved from wooden blocks instead of being built in clay. Of these, the one in the Juju house at Obudu may be taken as typical. Such bear the name Obo-Esa—the four hundred yams—and are specially raised as a means of increasing the crops.

When a fresh farm is cut, a special ceremony is carried out to induce the yam spirit to transfer its abode from the old farm to the new. The basket in which the great yam is contained, or post to which it is bound, is usually kept near a sapling of the tree which over the greater part of the West Coast is regarded as most sacred of all. This is a variety of Dolichandrone —strangely named considering the functions ascribed to it by natives—called by Kalabari Odumdum and by Ibo Ogrisi.

Among Ekoi, Efik and Ibibio, this beautiful tree with its glossy imparipinnate leaves and great clusters of pinkish-mauve flowers, is known as 'The Mother of the Town,' and a sapling of it is planted in nearly every compound. The finest specimen ever seen by us was found in one of the town playgrounds at Ikotobo in the Eket District.

Within the hollow trunk stood native pots filled with offerings, for to it come wives, young and old, to pray that 'plenty piccans' may be sent to bless their hearths. Hither, too, come ancient women to beg a like boon for their children and grandchildren. Should lightning shiver the ancient trunk or tornado strike it down, loud would be the wailing of those who had grown up beneath its shadow.[1]

It is unusual that trees of this species grow to such a size; yet very few compounds in the Ibo country are without a sturdy sapling, for not only its fertility-bestowing but also its purificatory powers are held in the utmost reverence. Should a Kalabari woman meet with vexation which causes her to shed tears while cooking her husband's food, it is thought that this will have ill results upon him unless, before serving it, she plucks some of the sacred leaves, draws them over her body and then strikes them upon the ground round about, that the evil effect of her tears may be negatived and her husband not suffer therefrom.

Not only is the Ajokko-Ji usually kept beneath the shelter of these sacred boughs, unless confided to the care of the ghosts in some ancestral shrine, but the Ogrisi itself becomes a symbol of the yam spirit. It was principally in this capacity, as emblem of the chief crop of the year, that at the death of each chief important enough to own an Obiri (reception room)—*i.e.* every head of a family of standing—a slave was killed as a sacrifice to the sacred tree.

Such unfortunate members of the community were well fed for several days, during which everything was done to cause them to be of good cheer and in perfect condition. Then they were robed in gay apparel and led forth to the sacred tree, where their throats were cut in such a manner that the blood flowed to the ground, fertilising the earth about its

[1] *Woman's Mysteries of a Primitive People* (Cassell), p. 81.

roots. No portion of such victims was ever eaten; their bodies were buried near by that thus Mother Ale might be enriched and induced to grant plentiful crops to those who brought her the offering.

The following information concerning the great Elele yam cult, Aya-Eke, was gleaned from Mr. D. Braid, for several years Native Court clerk of this town:

The compound where the Juju is kept is called Omo Kpurukpu and there, from election until death—at most seven years later, even should the full term of office be completed—the priest dwells, carefully guarded by all his people and never crossing the threshold unless called forth by some grave emergency. The reason for this restriction is that up to a few years ago any man who succeeded in killing the holder of this office would reign in his stead.

The whole prosperity of the town, especially the fruitfulness of farm, byre and marriage-bed, was linked with his life. Should he fall sick, it entailed famine and grave disaster upon the inhabitants, and there is reason to believe that, in such a case, facilities were offered to a successor. Under no circumstances did the term of office last for more than seven full years. This prohibition still holds; but since the coming of Government it is said that another of the same family, who must always be a strong man, may be chosen to take up the position in his stead. No sooner is a successor appointed, however, than the former priest is reported to ' die for himself.' It was frankly owned that, before Government came—*i.e.* some dozen years

ago—things were arranged differently in that, at any
time during his seven years' term, the priest might be
put to death by one strong and resourceful enough to
overcome him.

In answer to the question as to whether, in view of
the fate known to follow after so short a period, it was
not difficult to find men willing to succeed to the office
on such terms, Mr. Braid answered in a somewhat
surprised tone: ' Oh, no! Many wish for the post,
because so much wealth is brought them at the annual
festival that they become very rich—past all others in
the town.'

Our informant also stated that, during his own term
of office, Chief Eleche has only once been known to
pass beyond the compound walls. The occasion was
as follows:

A fellow townsman accused him of making a Juju
to kill the complainant. The case came into court
and, all unconscious of the excitement which such a
proceeding must cause, the chief was bidden to attend
and answer the charge. He arrived, accompanied by
nearly all the townsfolk, who not only filled the court-
yard, which is a very large enclosed space, but thronged
the market-place outside. They came, in a state
of great anxiety, to watch over the sacred priest and
guard him, so far as in them lay, from any misfortune
the effects of which, it was believed, would at once
react on all the countryside.

Doubtless Mr. Braid would have been less ready to
impart information of this nature, had it not been that
he was about to leave the place, in all probability never

to return, and had therefore nothing to fear from the townspeople. So soon as other official work allowed, I returned to Elele to adjust some difficulties which had meantime arisen, and also with the hope of gleaning further knowledge concerning Aya-Eke and its priest.

First I looked up the case in the course of which Eleche was summoned to appear. This was recorded under No. 353 and was heard on 7th December, 1914. It runs, in substance, as follows:

Yenanu, the plaintiff, stated on oath:

About two years ago I fell sick and the native doctors told me that people of my compound were trying to kill me. I therefore called a family meeting, in which the big men decided that Juju should be sworn for me. Eleche performed the ceremony, calling upon the Juju to slay anyone guilty of trying to bring about my death before new corn time. If this happened, they agreed to pay me four hundred manillas, four demi-johns of tombo, a basket of yams and a bottle of gin. Should no one die, it would prove that the accusation was untrue and I myself must pay the like amount in compensation for bringing a false charge. The time fixed upon had not expired when one of the men died, but I did not ask for payment.

Nine months after swearing Juju, the accused called me at Oka's compound and informed me that it was now young corn time ; yet no one had died, therefore I must pay the amount agreed upon. This I refused to do since one of them had been slain by the Juju. Then they conspired together and gave orders that I should be killed; also they put Juju in my well to prevent me and my people from getting water. Certain Jujus were also hung on the road to my farm by Eleche and Okuku. On this I went to Chief

Chioma and related the whole matter. He advised me not to eat any yams from the farm near which the Juju was placed. After this they ordered me to clean a portion of the road, but seeing that they were seeking to kill me I refused and went to work with Chief Chioma's people. After the road was finished, I was called before a meeting at Woda's house, where they ordered me to break down my compound and take all my properties to Chioma's quarter.

Oluene, witness for plaintiff, stated on oath:

I was present at the family meeting when the accused consulted together and made a rule that anyone who saw Yenanu should kill him ; nor did any of our people allow him to take fire, etc., from their houses.

The case was dismissed, but the complainant died soon after. Next Eke day, Eleche, wearing his Juju hat trimmed with seven eagle's feathers and the tail of a parrot, sallied forth, followed by all his people, to hold a progress throughout the town, while his attendants triumphantly proclaimed that Aya-Eke had slain the man who dared to summon her priest before mortal tribune.

On arrival at Elele our next step was to seek further information from the head men of the town, when these came to salute us. At first, the result was distinctly disappointing. No one had ever heard of the Juju or its priest! In fact, on the authority of all the principal inhabitants, no institution even remotely resembling Aya-Eke existed in the neighbourhood. Only after the case above quoted was shown to them did a light dawn upon the chiefs. Ah yes, they said, in very ancient days they believed there was some such

Juju in their town, but the memory of it had long since died away. As for Eleche, now they came to think of it, the priesthood had been in his family and possibly even he might hold that the office had descended to him. Since Government came to their country however—this with the most ingratiating smile—people had no use for such old superstitions, which had therefore fallen into utter neglect and forgetfulness. It was eagerly stated that there were other customs in their town much more worthy of the notice of the District Commissioner—for instance, Odo's Juju, the head priest of which was immediately found and brought forward. It would indeed be a pity, they added deferentially, should our time be wasted in enquiries into matters of so little account as those with which Eleche was concerned.

It was quite obvious that one and all were anxious to prevent further investigations and the result of the interview was naturally to send us hot-foot to the Omo-Kpurukpu quarter of the town, which is separated from the main section by some half mile of road. Here, in a house formed of elaborately carved wooden panels—to the best of my belief the only dwelling of its kind throughout the whole Division—lived the priest-king Eleche. Before the house stood a rude figure, formed of a stout post bound round with cloth, crowned with a cap and with two sticks extending arm-wise at right angles from near the top. This represented the late priest Eyinda, a brother of the present holder of the dignity, said to have died about two years ago.

Eleche himself wore a similar hat of office, its crown bound with a strip of white cloth, into which the seven emblematic eagle's feathers and the parrot's tail were fastened. He explained that he could not yet wear the full Juju dress of white baft, because he was not entitled to don this until after the third year of his priesthood, which period would not be ended before next harvest. His predecessors in the office, so far as his personal recollection went, had been named Eyinda, Omeneyin, Wana and Azunda. He himself had been a small boy when Azunda died. 'These,' said he, ' were great men of our house. Now of them all I alone am left to carry out the rites of the Juju, which is so powerful that death falls upon every man who offends against its laws.'

The rule of this Juju is very good, much like the law of the white men. By it, it is decreed, that no fighting or quarrelling, no seizure of property—above all, no shedding of blood—may take place upon Eke day.[1] No priest of Aya-Eke may eat of the new season's yams. All the harvest must be garnered and the festival held. Then, though others may eat, I may not until all the new farms have been cut and planted. Only when the last of the seed yams has been laid in the ground do the people bring me those which yet remain over in the yam racks. These I eat, calling the first of them ' my new season's yam ' though, in reality, it was garnered at the last harvest about seven moons before.

Our visit chanced to be paid at the beginning of April, and Eleche told us that nine days earlier he had eaten his first yam of the year.

[1] Eke day is one of the four days of the Ibo week. It is market day at Elele. Eke is also the name of the great python. See p. 7.

'All the people of Elele bring offerings to me,' he said. 'When the yams finish they bring plantains and I begin to chop those. Also they bring me much tombo. It is a very strong law of the Juju that no yams, save such as are old enough to plant, may be eaten by a priest of Aya-Eke. None has ever broken this rule ; for, should it be disobeyed, the seed yams would die in the ground, bearing no increase. All the great men of our family have kept the law faithfully. Now no more big men are left in our house; but I, though but a small boy in comparison with those powerful ones, also hold to this rule.'

Hereupon one of our party asked if he himself had power to appoint a successor, or in what way one was chosen. No sooner was the word 'successor' uttered than Eleche raised his arms over his head twice as though to ward off threatened danger, while his head wife, who kept close to him throughout, shrugged her shoulders violently over and over again, repeating in an agitated voice: 'Mba! Mba ! Che! Che!' (Let it not be! Let it not be!) Meanwhile the crowd of retainers took up the cry, low but angry, like the rumble of distant thunder, waving hands outward as if to drive off the ill-effects of such ominous speech. Eleche answered excitedly, the words tumbling over one another in his agitation:

'No successor is needed; for I shall never die! It is forbidden even to mention such a word! In the beginning of things, when I came out of the world, it was arranged that I should not be as other men but should live very long— looking after my people and bringing them prosperity. The fate of common men is not for me !' Thereupon, like a Greek chorus, came the response of the crowd: 'Oda! Oda! (Forbid it! Forbid it!)

The head wife, who had seated herself so soon as her husband did so, although all the others remained standing at a respectful distance, was a youngish woman evidently holding a position of more than usual importance. Later, we learned that it was customary for this head wife to die ' about the same time as her husband ' ; but all attempts to extract more definite information were met with professions of ignorance.

The most important ceremonies of the cult are held at the time of the new yam harvest, when a great sacrifice is made and, as already mentioned, every man, woman and child of Elele brings a gift to the house of the priest. Before leaving, we asked whether no other rites were observed in honour of Aya-Eke and were told that early in May, *i.e.* at the beginning of the rainy season, all the inhabitants gathered to witness a wrestling match held in the open space before Eleche's house. This is continued on every big Eke day, *i.e.* each eighth day, for about three months until the new yam festival, during which the feast of the ancestral spirits is also celebrated. Later, all go to Chief Woyike's compound in the Omopo quarter and there wrestle in honour of the new corn Juju, Mbara (Lord of the Town), of which he is priest. After his festival is over, all wrestling finishes for the year.

No sooner had we learned this than we set out for the new shrine. Here, at the opposite extremity of the town, lies the compound known as Obakere, inhabited by Woyike, priest of the rival Juju. The chief received us with simple friendliness and seemed

Fig. 44.   Chief Eleche with his head wife, standing by memorial
            pillar of the late Head Priest of Aya-Eke

willing for a visit to his shrine. Nor, after the first
shyness had worn off, did he show any reluctance to
speak of the Juju, concerning which a few carefully-
careless questions brought out the following information:

When the wrestling at Eleche's is finished, all men come
here to witness mine; after which the whole town must
cease from such contests, which may not be held again till
the next season comes round. We think that this ceremony
will help the crops to grow strong, overcoming evil influences
and bearing much increase. The reason why the wrestling
is held first at Eleche's place and then mine, is that his Juju
Aya-Eke is wife to my Juju 'Mbara. The first is feminine
and looks after the yams; mine is male, the spirit of corn.
When the first green shoot pushes through the soil, I make
ready and, on the coming of the young cobs, my Juju pro-
claims a four months' peace. During this time no one may
fight with another nor seize any person or property. Should
a man offend against this rule six manillas and a goat must
be paid to revoke the Juju for him, otherwise he would
die.

When the time comes round, I go forth and announce
that if anyone does anything to annoy the Juju I will not
allow him to take part in my ceremony. To me no gifts
are brought like those borne every year to Eleche; but when
the season comes round I make a great feast for the people,
giving them much food and palm-wine in abundance.

The priest was old and somewhat worn-looking.
Round his shrunken ankles were bound little bones,
pierced through at either end and fastened by black
cord in three rows. These, he said, were a powerful
medicine to keep off rheumatics and other ills which
beset the aged, but had nothing to do with his Juju.

'How indeed could such a thing be possible,' he queried,

> since 'Mbara is a male Juju and the bones are those of Tortoise, who, as is well known, is proper only to feminine cults? By the place where I usually sit a tortoise was impaled years ago for protection; then, when it was decayed enough, I took the little bones out from the shell and, after they had been cleaned, strung them into these anklets, as you see. There are three Ale shrines in our town, by each of which Tortoise is impaled. Also before the shrine of Aya-Eke a shell may naturally be seen.

Towards the middle of May we found ourselves back again in Elele and enquiries brought out the fact that the first wrestling of Aya-Eke was to be held about noon on the morrow. The hour seemed a strange one to choose for such a purpose, under a tropical sun; but before mid-day drums began to beat in the distance, summoning the people with the unmistakable rhythm only used for such occasions. So soon therefore as court was over, we set out to follow the call.

It was 15th May and a day of blazing sunshine; yet crowds had already collected and sat, the elect in a circle many deep round the compound, while the rest almost blocked the road along its front. Three sets of drums were playing; first Eleche's household band, secondly one supplied by a neighbouring quarter, and thirdly, just before the shrine, that which bore the proud name of 'The Juju's Own.' This consisted of six drums, three tall and upright, three long and oval.

Opposite the door of the principal shrine a little group of offerings was to be seen, backed by the

branched sticks of the Thunder God. Questioned as
to this, Eleche said:

> Amade Onhia is kin to my Juju. In many towns the
> biggest Jujus have the habit of sending to request him to
> come and stay by them. Aya-Eke did this and ordered
> that his shrine should be placed opposite to her own, saying
> that when ceremonies were made in her honour they should
> be performed for him also. On being asked as to when the
> wrestling would begin, Eleche answered, with true African
> placidity, that this depended upon the arrival of the com-
> batants, who would probably not appear until the sun sank
> lower in the heavens. He explained that he had told us
> the play began at mid-day, because by ancient custom the
> summoning drums must start at that time.

Now, according to widespread West Coast belief,
noon and midnight are the special times at which ghosts
walk abroad. Among Ibo and Kalabari little
children are warned never to throw sticks or stones
when the sun is high overhead, lest they should
inadvertently injure one of these wandering spirits
and thus draw down its wrath upon themselves.
With Mbolli and Etche Ibo—as usually in the Ikwerri
country—seed yams and corn are stored in the shrine
of the ancestors, *i.e.* beneath the guardianship of these
beneficent friends, much as was the seed-grain of
ancient Rome within the sacred Mundus. Chief
Eleche also told us that the Egu Nda Madu, the
festival of the forefathers, is always held at the same
time as that of the new yams and, were these rites
neglected, the ghosts would cease to exert a protective
influence upon the next season's crops. It is probable,
therefore, that the reason the drums must start to play

at noonday is to call the attention of the ancestral shades
to the fact that the ritual wrestling is about to begin.

First, one or two youths stepped out, at long
intervals, from the ranks of patient spectators, to dance
round in wide circles, always from left to right—in the
contrary direction to the hands of a clock.   Later, as
the shadows lengthened, more and more joined in the
pastime, till from twenty to thirty were dancing almost
continuously.   Nearly all raised eyes and hands to
heaven at a point, roughly speaking, halfway round
the circle.   Most of the performers wore necklets
of knotted palm, while a considerable number bore
in addition a single vivid bloom of the scarlet Akpane
Besin—the old Ekoi wrestlers' challenge—stuck in
their black locks.

In the midst of the circle danced a strange figure,
wearing a tail of skin behind and a long strip of blue
native cloth falling before.   Round his waist was a
girdle of brass bells; a band of cowries, three deep,
was fastened beneath the knee, while a cloth of leaf-
green silk was tightly bound round the loins.   In his
right hand he bore a horn, black and twisted like that
of a bushbuck, the open end filled with a tassel of long
fur.   This, when stationary, he sometimes drove
point downwards into the earth or, while circling round
with the other dancers, bore it raised over his head.
Chief Yellow explained that such was the traditional
wrestlers' costume.

During the dances several ' masters of ceremonies,'
bearing bunches of palm-leaves, went up and down,
keeping a clear space—driving back the circle of

FIG. 45.   Wrestling to make the yams grow.   Chief Eleche's place, Elele

spectators by striking these on legs and feet. Suddenly the performers scattered, leaving two of their number alone in the centre. These bent and touched the ground with their fingers, then almost immediately gripped and after a struggle, which caused the wildest excitement among the spectators, the taller and slighter of the two flung the other to earth and seated himself firmly astride the prostrate form—to be lifted upon the shoulders of a friend and thus borne round amid the plaudits of the multitude.

So it went on, couple after couple struggling till one was overthrown. Occasionally, if they were deemed ill matched or thought to be growing angry, friends rushed in, as is usual in such contests, to separate the combatants. What struck us as unusual was the short time allowed to each pair. Should one not succeed in throwing the other after the first few minutes the spectators flung themselves between and bore them apart by force. This was explained to be ' lest they should become exhausted,' and was possibly done with the idea that such a result might, by sympathetic magic, have an ill effect upon the crops.

These wrestling rites are carried out amongst nearly all the Ibo in the Division, though held in greatest importance among the Ikwerri. The same ceremony is customary with the Mbolli, whose head chief told us: ' When the season comes round for the festival of Mbiencha,[1] we make sacrifice to her of fowls and goats. After the sacrifice has been made, we start wrestling. We do this for children, farms and health.'

[1] Mbiencha is the child of Nkike, the Mbolli Earth Goddess.

One evening, during our stay at Elele, we heard the sound of a far-off tom-tom, beaten with a queer insistent call. The method of playing was new to us, so without a word to any one we set out to investigate. There was no need to ask the way, since it was easy enough to follow the beat of the drum. This led through the market-place along the Omo Dioga road; then, after a sharp turn to the right, we found ourselves in an open space, upon one side of which trees tossed dark branches against a sky of scuttling cloud.

The moon, nearing her third quarter, was climbing up the heavens, shedding a cloud of misty silver radiance upon the scene beneath. By a fortunate chance our shoes fell soundlessly upon the soft sand; so we stole in unnoticed, shadows amid a multitude of shadows which flitted to and fro ' now in glimmer and now in gloom '—in swaying, everchanging lines of a dance impossible to describe.

My companions were wearing white, as was nearly every woman and most of the men present. The latter mostly wore long flowing Hausa robes, bought or imitated from the fashion set by Chief Ododo, the enterprising Hausa who, following in the steps of a mighty elephant-hunter of his race, settled here and made himself chief of the town.

At once, on realising what was going forward, we slipped into a pool of shadow, cast, it seemed, expressly for our convenience in a spot where we could see everything but ourselves passed for a while unnoticed.

Men and women danced in separate lines, approaching and retreating. To our surprise we saw that many of the latter wore not only white robes but white coiffures as well; for their crisp, dark wool was covered with a dressing of native chalk or pale-tinted clay, while the faces were often streaked with white lines, giving them an appearance indescribably ghost-like. To and fro, backward and forward, co-mingling at one moment and the next in clearly defined lines, moved the dancers to the monotonous tom-toming of their strange orchestra, which somehow managed to suggest things beyond the power of words—the fall of the first rains upon the parched earth; the enfolding of soft mists, from whose gentle embrace springs a stirring and quickening, changing her barrenness into fruition; the swelling of grain and root crops in the dark ground; the first feeble upward striving of young shoots, later to spring into radiant verdure in the free air above; the passion of pride, of life and strength and love—all that is poignantly felt but can seldom be expressed save perhaps by the monotonous beat of the tom-tom, the strange soughing of elephant horns and thrumming of savage lyres on such a night as this.

Only one air evolved by a northern musician gives any idea of the effect of these weird African melodies—that is the Braut March in *Lohengrin*, which, written on so few notes, yet beats with a strange persistence on certain fibres of the human instrument. In this, too, the theme is much the same—the bringing of the Earth Bride to the arms of her mystic bridegroom. Each thema, monotonous in itself, changed imperceptibly into another equally monotonous but built on different notes and shadowing forth a very infinitude of meaning.

In and out among the dancers crept strange shapes, elaborately coiffured and with whitened faces, much in the style of some Ibo masks, at the time of unknown origin, which wandered into our collection several years ago. These have since been explained as typifying the moon, much after the manner of the so-called Isis masks of the Pangwe Moon Goddess So; or again as representing those strange wanderers from the ghost realm, the spirits of beneficent ancestors who watch over the harvests of their descendants.

Hardly daring to breathe, we watched the strange phantasmagoric figures pass to and fro in the intricate mazes of the dance—the lines merging and separating in oozy triangles, squares and circles such as those woven by Ka for the perdition of the Banda Log.

Suddenly a change came over the scene. The tom-toms sounded a series of sharp insistent strokes. The moon, emerging from friendly clouds, shed a brilliant light upon the place where we had hitherto remained hidden in shadow, and the crowd, grown aware of our presence, began to scatter. We withdrew with all possible speed since nothing further was to be learnt by delay. After our departure the mystic dance began once more and continued, as could be heard from the far-away drumming, almost till the first rays of dawn.

On 26th July chance led us to pass by Chief Eleche's compound while a ceremony connected with the Aya-Eke cult was in progress. Under the Obiri shed, a

band of various drums, together with a particularly
sweet-toned xylophone formed of cork-wood slabs laid
upon fresh-cut plantain stems, was playing. To the
sound of this music danced the chief of Elele Aliminni
(Ale by the water) with his three principal wives.
Two points were specially noticeable in the per-
formance; first, the intense solemnity of the dancers,
and, secondly, the way in which their oneness of
purpose was emphasised by gesture. This is the only
West African dance witnessed by us in which the
performers continually linked arms, or twined these
round one another's shoulders and waists.

When Chief Eleche was questioned as to the meaning
of the ceremony, he said that it was performed in order
to draw down the blessing of the great Juju Aya-Eke
on the chief of Elele Aliminni, his family and crops,
before beginning to dig the first yams of the year.

A few weeks later came one of the greatest dis-
appointments of our tour. By means of much
planning it had been made possible, though with
considerable difficulty, to arrive at Elele on the day
before that fixed for the great yam festival, which we
were anxious to witness. As ill fortune would have
it, however, a runner came in in the late afternoon to
bring tidings of trouble which was thought likely to
break out in a far-off corner and to prevent which the
presence of the white man was needed. To hesitate
under such circumstances was of course naturally
impossible. So the crowning ceremony of the year,
the Aya-Eke harvest festival, was perforce missed.

IX

ALE AND THE ANCESTORS

ANOTHER link between Ale and her human children may be found at Ogu, a town inhabited by Okrikans, in the extreme east of the District. Here marriage is only solemnised once a year, immediately before the making of new farms. The Earth Goddess, locally called Amakiri (Earth of the town) is the principal deity, and not far to the rear of her shrine stands that of Ababa, the protectress of marriage. The spot sacred to the latter is an oval enclosure, fenced round by a wall of rough logs. Within this grow many Odumdum—the tree which, as previously mentioned, is looked upon almost all over the West Coast as bestower of babes, protector against evil influences and purifying agent, as well as in some cases the symbol of the yam spirit and that of the Earth Goddess herself.

Thither, before the cutting of new farms, go all the brides of the year to take the vow of faithfulness to their new-made lords. Libations of rum and palm wine are poured out, while the blessing of the indwelling Genius, Tenye Te'en, is invoked upon the faithful and her vengeance called down upon any woman who should prove false to her wedded vows.

In the local shrine of Obaji (or Obazi) the god of the

sea, we came across a representation of multiplied, or limitless, birth—eight frogs carved from a solid strip of wood. Several other slabs showed designs of the sacred crocodile with human beings laid out before it in sacrifice.

A frog is often depicted—with probably the same reason—in the carved tablets known as Nyama Ahia or sometimes Ahia Osimiri (the river market), which are hung up as ghost offerings in Ikwerri Ibo houses in order to remind the ancestral spirits of the need for constant activity in increasing the prosperity of their descendants. In one found at Elele, the sacred crocodile and the phallic serpent are shown together with the hoe, the symbol of fruitful Ale. Again, the central figure has its tail joined to another hoe, while the tail of the serpent touches that of the crocodile and is thereby linked with the hoe.

Fig. 46. Ancestral Tablet

During the making and planting of farms among Mbolli and Abuan—both tribes of particular interest and distinct type—the rule of strict chastity must be observed. No man may approach his wife until his share of the work is over. The labour apportioned to the males of the tribe at this season consists, first, in cutting and firing bush, after which women clear away the charred branches. Men again usually dig the holes into which it is the task of maids and matrons to lay the yam tubers.   Nowadays, however, both the last mentioned duties fall to the lot of women.   Till every ' seed of Proserpine ' has been laid in the dark ground, however, neither wife nor maid may yield to the prayer of husband or lover; for should the strictest chastity fail to be practised during this period, the farm of the frail one would yield but scanty increase.

Among Mbolli, in the words of the Chief Igwe of Ogali:

> We worship our ancestors (Okwenji).   We sacrifice to them fowl and fish.   Rich men give goats at such times. The sacrifices are made three times a year—at the harvests; first at the new corn month, next one month later again and then five months later, when we start digging yams.   We hold this festival in the tenth month (November) and go to cut farm again two months later.   We start to count months from putting the crops in the ground till we begin to dig—*i.e.* ten moons.
>
> At the feast of the ancestors we pour out drink, saying:
> ' Ebe   atena   'mgbom   ami,   ami   'mgbo   nan   mwi.'
> ' As   (my) father   got   me,   (let) me   get   other   child.'
>
> We have already lived two moons in the farm—October and November.   We shall stop another five.   While we stay in the farms, we may not have connection with our wives; for such a thing we must come back to the town, sleep for a night and then go back.   Otherwise we should offend 'Nkike, who would not let our crops grow well or send plenty children.

Among the Ale Nsaw Ibo a strict rule as to chastity was imposed by the direct command of the Earth Goddess.   On this point Chief Osu of Obiakpo stated:

Fig. 47.   Shrine of Ojuku juju at Woji

Our people are generally known by the name of Ale 'Nsaw (Ale's tabu or the land of the tabu) because in our ancestors' time there were many forbidden things in our part. All our women were sacred to Ale, therefore in olden days no man might reach out a hand to touch a woman's leg or foot. Should a man meet a woman going to bush, he must at once hide his eyes or pass by another way. In those days it was a very terrible sin for any man to commit adultery. Should one fall into this crime, he was not only heavily fined but at once made outcast. Never again was he permitted to join any 'company.' Never again might he drink or eat with others. As regarded his own family, because he was of their kin they would help to collect the fine, but after this was paid off they would have nothing further to do with him.

Among the Abuan, who live to the west of the Sombreiro River, the law of the Earth Mother as to chastity is even more strictly enforced. Like the Mbolli, this people on starting the new season's farms early in January, take up their abode in little huts built on their plantations. There they spend the space of three months, after which they return to their town for about four weeks, and then go back for another three months, weeding the crops and tending them till they grow strong for harvest.

During all that time strict continence obtains. It is absolutely forbidden for any man to approach a woman, *even his own wife*. Should desire prove too strong, the pair must leave their farm and seek their town dwelling for the purpose. Any breach of this law is thought to have disastrous effect upon the crops.

Again, while, as already mentioned, it is regarded throughout the whole of the region as a grave sin against the Earth Mother for a woman to yield to the embraces of any man, whether lover or husband, while lying upon the ground, the crime is of yet deeper dye if committed upon farm land than in the depth of the bush.   In olden days a couple convicted of such an offence would have little chance of surviving the wrath of their outraged townsfolk.   Even now such a charge would bring down upon the accused the invocation of some reputedly fatal Juju.   For instance, in a case heard at Abua Court (No. 116/14), a woman named Ugenni stated as follows:

> All our townspeople laughed at me, saying that I was having connections with men under plantains.   So I said, whoever accused me of having connections under plantains, the Juju Obuku of Amingbokko must kill that person.

The same law against intercourse in the bush— and in some parts in a canoe—prevails throughout almost the entire Niger Delta.   Among the Jekri it is so strong that in a recent murder case (Rex versus Iyeabor) it came out that the dead woman had such belief in the strength of this tabu—and an additional one which enjoined chastity during pregnancy—that she had no hesitation in going into the bush with her murderer, a man whom she knew to be desirous of her.

Case No. 297 tried in the Ijaw Native Court of Nembe in January, 1925, gives the procedure which was adopted in order to convert a ' bush ' place, where cohabitation was not allowed, into a village, where this could take place with impunity.

Igoin and his people sometimes stayed at this newly discovered place for two months, but no cohabitation was to be conducted there. One of the main reasons why they used to return to Nembe was because no husband was allowed to use his wife as regards sexual intercourse there.

Finally an envoy was sent to the Long Juju (that of Aro Chuku)—a journey which would have taken at least several weeks—' to ask for the necessary ceremony to be performed on the village, so that one can have connection with his own wife. Alegi returned from the Long Juju and told Ogede the rites which should be carried out. Ogede performed the necessary ceremony. The ceremony he performed was first he let a cock and hen cohabit at Ewelesuo. He brought one thing called ' Ovo ' (Covenant) from Long Juju, one ' Odo ' (a red round stuff) and a round white lime and gave these to the juju to appease the jujus and prayed that the village should become an inhabitable town and that one can have connection with his wife. Before this ceremony was performed it was forbidden for a woman to urinate in the village (Ewelesuo). On this account one place was chosen and called ' Sanpogu ' *i.e.* (Waterside for urine).

' Egula and Ogede were friends. After the ceremony had been performed Egula went after his friend and settled at Ewelesuo. Egula was dancing a juju called ' Akpana.' This juju Akpana and those at Ewelesuo made a covenant and Egula then ' danced '

juju at Ewelesuo. Eugla is a native doctor. Ogeda
asked the juju, when Egula was dancing it, why they
are not allowed to remain at Ewelesuo in November
month. The juju asked whether he will be able to
do so. He said ' Yes.' The juju then told him that,
if people wanted to remain at Ewelesuo in November
month, the people should keep a watch-night in the
town and when the water ebb, they (the people)
should take all jujus to the water edge and let the water
soak them—which signifies that all the juju has gone
out of the town (Oru iderimo). Then when December
came the whole inhabitants should man one canoe,
beat the tom-tom and sing a song and go to a creek
called ' Orumokolo.' A prophet native doctor was
to be in the canoe who will say to the people in the
canoe that the jujus had come in. Then the canoe is to
return to the town (Oru iwomo) and a juju called
Ogoni is to be danced. Ogede agreed to perform all
these. They (the people) were then to dance on
three consecutive days after these jujus have been
performed.'

In many parts of the country there is likewise a
strong tabu against the commission of adultery,
particularly in the husband's or adulterer's house, and
against a woman cooking food for her husband when
she has just returned from her lover.

No sooner is farm work finished, however, than, as
already stated, scenes of licence are not only permitted
over the greater portion of this region, but even
enforced in certain parts; for, just as the priestesses
of some temples of old Greece were obliged to offer

themselves to strangers, so excesses, regarded as most reprehensible at other periods, are encouraged at this.

Among certain of the Brass Ijaw adultery is openly condoned under certain conditions. It is the custom, for some towns that are friendly together, to make an agreement that no man will take an action in Court against any other of their inhabitants and claim damages or punishment for adultery.

This plea was raised in case No. 253/25 before Amassama Native Court and an action for damages was dismissed in view of a covenant to this effect between the towns of Amassama and Agoro.

The cult, in which religious prostitution was perhaps most openly and extensively practised throughout the Ibo country, was that of Ife-Ala (literally ' thing of Ala ' or ' that which concerns Ala ').

To those few Europeans, who have hitherto had knowledge of this cult, it appears to have been known as the Ifallum Juju. All natives questioned on the subject, however, including Chief Gabriel Yellow, stated that the real name was as above given. The headquarters of this particular cult of the Earth Goddess were at Nguru, a town to the North of Okpala in Owerri Division:

> All people from neighbouring lands went there and lodges were also set up in nearly all important towns throughout Degama District. Many men and women, who could not be cured from trouble by native doctors, went there to pray

for help, but the priest refused to invoke the aid of the Juju unless the suppliant brought him a virgin as gift.   The priest then took her as handmaid and she was kept in the temple and hired out by him to worshippers—especially to sterile men who came to pray for increased virility.   Such ' slaves of the Juju ' were marked out by a shaven patch at the top of the head.

There were about three hundred of these girls at Nguru but to none of them was it permitted to rear a babe, because by native custom they would have been obliged to refrain from the company of men for the two years during which they were suckling their offspring—and this would naturally have greatly diminished their earnings.   So soon as a babe was born, therefore, the law of the Juju ordained that it must be disposed of in one of two ways ;   either must it be clubbed on the head and flung away, or laid in one of the big earthen jars and deposited in the bush beyond the town.

The Nguru lodge was suppressed about 1913 by Mr. J. M. Binny, District Commissioner.   Great was the joy of the three hundred women thus set free to rear the babes born to them, instead of being forced to slay these at the harsh behest of the covetous priest of Ale.

A belief in the efficacy of sacrificial blood in order to purchase the favour of the powers of fertility is world-wide; but perhaps nowhere in past days did this dread libation flow in such streams as in West Africa. It is true that now the vigilance of Government and missionary effort have succeeded, to a great extent, in substituting that of slaughtered fowls, sheep and goats, for the costly ichor drawn from mortal veins; but in many a hidden shrine on the banks of unexplored creeks or in the depths of the silent bush—wherever indeed a chance occurred to do so in secret—human victims were till lately offered up.   Especially was this practised at the season when the yam vines first send forth tender shoots to clothe the poles with green— as a means towards strengthening the new crops—and at harvest, in gratitude to Ale for her bountiful gifts of garnered grain.   At such times it was dangerous for any unprotected wayfarer to venture forth beyond the borders of his own country, since strangers were very liable to seizure for such a purpose.   Kula, the centre of many strange and terrible cults, bore an ominous reputation in this respect, until its evil practices drew the attention of Government and, as a result, the principal shrines were destroyed.

In May of one year, a chief stated, they chanced to sacrifice a Brass woman.   I do not know how she managed to disappear from her own town, but the Kula people caught her for their Juju.   Always they made sacrifice when the new yams were coming up from the ground.   Every Juju of every nation demands a victim at that time of year.   News of the sacrifice of this Brass woman was brought to Mr. Binny when he was D.C. of Degama; so he went down and destroyed that Juju house.   Word went forth that it was to be burnt to the ground, whereon the people came to him and said: ' May we not take the sticks of which it is made to mend our own compounds ? '   Therefore he gave permission and the townsfolk pulled it down themselves. In the shrine were found many skulls carved from wood in exact imitation of real human skulls. There too were human figures, finely painted; some like those modelled in clay in the 'Mbari houses and others like the 'Nduen Fobara (ancestral images) in Kalabari shrines.

Yet another link between ancestor worship and that of the Earth Mother Ala is to be found at Omo-Ala (children of Ala)—a town in the south-eastern part of the Division which proved to be a great centre both of the cult of the Earth Goddess and of the forefathers.

Here, as in most other Ibo towns, nearly every compound has its sacred tree which is usually a specimen either of Ojji (*Chlorophora excelsa*) or Oil Bean (*Pentaclethra macrophylla*). In this the souls of the departed are thought to dwell while awaiting reincarnation. So long as the least fragment of the tree lasts, the faithful shades cling to its ancient trunk or branches or even retire into the furthermost rootlets. For this reason, when one of these giants falls beneath Time's axe, the family to which it belongs marks the place where it formerly stood and no farm may be made thereon again. Were this not done, it is thought that the ghosts might be imprisoned for ever since they could not break through the earth to return to the light of day, lest, by so doing, they might injure the sown crops of Ale.

Before the last rootlets of the ' ghost trees ' return to the dust of Mother Ale, the spirits announce to their family through the mouth of some medicine man that a new tree must be chosen for their dwelling-place. The homes of such ancestral shades are obvious, even to the most careless passer-by, from the earthen pots or bowls and the freshly-offered plantains, etc., which may always be found amid the roots.

At the planting of new farms the members of each compound assemble beneath the family tree and give a great play.   At such times they bring gifts and dance and sing, robed in their best, praying the ancestral shades to guard the seeds laid in the bosom of Mother Earth and help them to come to fruition.   Again, at harvest time, another play is held to thank the ghosts for their share of the crops.   A part of the increase is always set aside in gratitude to these beneficent spirits.

There is an interesting point to be noted about such ' ghost trees.'   In this part of the District only the souls of good men are thought to await reincarnation in these peaceful dwelling-places, gladdened by sunshine, quickened by gentle dews or warm fertilising rain and refreshed by soft breezes.   It is a matter of firm belief that, however fiercely tornados may rage around, these are spared.   The branches of such trees are never rudely torn nor dashed together, while no thunderbolt has ever been hurled against their sacred trunks.

The ghost of an evil man would in vain seek admittance within the shelter of the family tree, but would be driven forth by the shades of his blameless kin to await, in animal form, a new term of earth life.

Young brides, therefore, often linger beneath those trees in which dwell the souls of gentle ancestors, in the hope that one such may choose her as his Janua terrae. Among Owerri Ibo, however, a different belief is held; only the ghosts of those foully slain, whether by force or witchcraft, are thought to seek refuge in the tree tops, there to wail and cry throughout the hours of darkness and in time of storms with a pitiful sound ' like a small chick or a piccan but a few days old,' until the guilty cause of their untimely death has been brought to justice.

It has already been mentioned that ghosts, who have taken on brute form while awaiting reincarnation, sometimes fall upon women who chance to pass through their haunts.   By means of the animal body, which they temporarily inhabit, these evil spirits force their unfortunate victims to bear a babe, into which the sinful soul may enter—thus procuring an earlier return to mortal state.

From a case heard in Degama Native Court it also transpired that, among some Kalabari at least, the belief is held that the spirits of dead husbands are not altogether cut off from earthly joys but, when bound by specially ardent affection for the wives they have left behind, may on occasion return for the purpose of once more embracing the object of their desire. That such a proceeding is supposed to be not without danger to the woman thus visited will be seen from the statement of Ogoloba H. Horsfall, who summoned her brother-in-law, Charlie H. Horsfall, for accusing her of witchcraft.   Complainant stated on oath:

Three months ago the defendant accused me of witchcraft. This was on the Government beach.   He stated that several people had died in the house owing to my having bewitched them. My husband was defendant's brother. He died, and since his death has appeared to me in the night time and tried to have connection with me. I had to make medicine to stop this, as otherwise I might have died.

How deeply the longing for offspring is ingrained in the hearts of these people may be gauged to a certain extent by the horror of the means to which they will sometimes resort in order to overcome sterility or increase fruitfulness. For such an end no crime is too cruel; no magic rite too dark or revolting. For example, a case was reported from the Ogoni country on unimpeachable authority but seven years ago, in which the foetus was removed from a pregnant woman in order to be shared out among, and devoured by, others who believed this to be a sure way of increasing fertility.

In a land case, which had arisen between the Okrikans and the Mbolli tribe and came before me in April 1915, it was stated by Daniel Kalio, head chief of the former, that the disputed territory had been seized by his people in punishment for the terrible crime committed by their opponents.

In the old days, he said, the river formed the boundary between our land; but our women were in the habit of crossing over to attend the markets. One day, while thus peacefully buying and selling, the 'Mbolli rose and slew seventy-two of them at one time—forty-one at one place and thirty-one at another. Their heads were struck off and borne before the Juju; while the bodies of those who had been about to bear babes were slashed open and the small, small piccans removed and carried away.

It was suggested from another source that this last outrage was promoted by the same idea as that recorded among their neighbours the Ogoni and that the Mbolli sought, by this terrible means, to procure unprecedented fruitfulness to their own women. The suggestion, however, has never been substantiated.

The story of the coming of Ale was told by an Ibo named Obi Amara. It differs from the usual southern Ikwerri Ibo idea that Chi, or Chineke, the creatrix, was the great first cause from which all mortal men have sprung. He explained seeming contradictions by saying that to Ale the bodies alone were due, into which Chi sent down souls from the Spirit Realm.

They make Ale play for this country at the feast of new yams and also give food to Ale when they want plenty yams, especially at the sowing of farms. Ale is the mother of all Ibo people. Her husband is called 'Ndiche.

Perhaps it is worth mentioning here that this was the only occasion on which any such appellation was given among the many local names for the spouse of Ale. Ndiche, or Ndichie, itself is the ordinary Ibo word for the forefathers, and the relationship here mentioned between the Earth Goddess and these beneficent shades is significant in view of the co-operation thought to exist between them, not only as regards seed corn and harvest but also fertility of the hearth. Further it may be noticed that the primary cause of the coming of Ale, as here given, was not to provide a home for the living but a resting place for the dead. To continue:

There is a big bird in our country named Ogbughu (hornbill). Its mother died. In those days Ale was not, so that the bird could find no place to bury his mother. He went round and round and at last had to bury her on his own head. That is why he bears upon his head a mound the shape of a grave to the present day. After a while, as he flew over the water, seeking a resting-place but finding none, he saw one fine woman and one man swimming in the water. As he watched, he saw they were making something and, in a short time, the first land began to appear. When it had grown quite big, Ale cried : ' When any man dies, let him be brought and buried here.' Her own body she stretched over the land; she it is who made all, both the earth and the earth-folk, whom she bore from her womb. When the dead are buried they turn to earth, so that our people say: ' We are of one body with Ale.' The trees too she brought. Ojji tree was the first that ever grew upon earth. The second was Agbo (or Akpu, the silk cotton tree) and the third Odala. Food is still given to this tree for every child which is born to a house and, if a woman wants a piccan, she brings a fowl to the Odala tree.

When a woman wants to become a mother, she lies down to sleep for night time after prayer to Ale. She dreams that Odala brings a piccan and lays it upon her breast. At daybreak she wakes and cries: ' Where is the piccan that was over my heart ? ' Then she takes a long piece of chalk,[1] called 'Nsu by Ibos, and lays it before the Odala tree, praying: ' Make my dream come true.'

The fourth tree which Ale brought was the Kola Ojji, the fruit of which is often set out in offering to the ghosts. At an Ale feast the women bring food and the oldest man of the town offers it up. After a man has eaten of such a feast,

[1] This offering is of the same shape, though apparently slightly larger than the small phallic symbols found before the Juju Ezum Mezum depicted on p. 92.

should he do any evil thing that day, Ale would surely kill him.

When a bad sickness comes upon a town, the old priest of Ale, who is always the head chief, beats upon the long drum to call all the people together in order to find out the cause of the trouble. Then Kola nuts are laid upon the place set apart for offerings. Each man in turn kneels down and picks up the kola with his lips, eats it and goes away. This is done until the guilty one comes. When a wizard bends down to take Ale's kola, the Earth Spirit catches him and he is forced by her power to. confess how he spread the pestilence. Before all the people he must speak out, saying: ' I killed this man. I killed that man. That woman also I slew ! '—until all his crimes are known. When everything has been told, his belly swells up and he dies. No man touches him. It is by Ale's power alone that he is slain.

This aversion to witchcraft is characteristic not only of the Earth Mother but also of her spouse the Thunder God; for, though certain magicians can raise a tempest by their spells, it is held to be extremely dangerous for witch or wizard to practise magic rites during the time of storms. When a man is struck by lightning, it is thought that Amade Onhia slew him on account of his crimes. Such men are never buried, lest the evil within them should defile Ale. The corpses are therefore flung away into the bush of the unblest dead. Similarly among Aro and some other Ibo tribes no tree struck by lightning can be used for firewood; since food cooked upon this would be accursed and even the light and heat given out by such logs would have a sinister influence on all whom it might reach.

With these peoples the bed-rock of religious ideas has perhaps been attained in this direction; and, unless the fascination of the subject has misled one with will-o'-the-wisp-like glamour, then surely in the cult of the Earth Mother, of the Sky Father, by whose fecundative showers her fruition is brought about, of the kindly ancestors, whose spirits still watch over their descendants and aid in the sending of rich harvests—lastly, and most intimately of all, by sympathetic magic through that mysterious link thought to lie between the generative organs, both male and female, and the fruitfulness of the animal and vegetable kingdoms—the innermost workings of primitive minds may, in a measure, be reached at last.

INDEX

A

Abara, messenger of the Earth Goddess: represented in Mbari Houses, 16-7.

Abaw, clan of Ika sub-tribe of Ibo : 79.

Abuan, Semi-Bantu tribe : 75, 121, 123.

Adultery: Tabus 126-7 ; condonation of 127.

Ajiji, ' play ' 93-4.

Ajokko-ji, or Njokku : Yam cult 99 *et seq.* ; among Mbolli 29.

Ala, or Ale, or Ana. *See* Earth Goddess.

Ale Nsaw, sub-tribe of Ibo : 122-3.

Amade Onhia, or Amad'ongha. *See* God of Lightning.

Ancestors : and Fertility 9, 60, 113, 120 ; and Ale 120 *et seq.* esp. 134 ; accursed 64 ; shrines and phallic figures 84 ; symbols 80-1 ; between reincarnations 77, 130-2.

Ant-hill : and phallic cults 90-2.

Ape : represented in Mbari Houses 22, 24-5.

Aro, sub-tribe of Ibo ; and worship of Thunder God 46.

Art : clay figures in Mbari Houses 15, 41.

Axe, double-headed : depicted on Ikoro drum 4, 8.

B

Binny, Mr. J. M., former District Commissioner 108-9.

Bird and Pillar worship 43.

Birth : representation in Mbari Houses 15, 24, 51 ; due to Jujus 60.

Blood and Fertility 102, 128-9.

Burial. *See* Death.

C

Chief of town : must be priest of Ale 12.

Child birth : Tabus re 63.

Coiffure : representations in Mbari Houses 15, 41.

Cooking cones. *See* Eku 82 *et seq.*

Copulation : method of 24-5 ; with the dead 132 ; unnatural 33-6 ; Tabus re 32-3, 121 *et seq.* ; and cults of Earth Goddess and Thunder God 15, 48.

Crocodile : depicted on Ikoro drum etc. 4, 7, 9.

Cult, yam 99 *et seq. See* Fertility.

D

Dance, at Elele : 116 *et seq.*

Death : Tabus re 62-4.

Drum, the Great : 1 *et seq.*

E

Earth. *See* Goddess. Spousals with Sky 61.

Egyptians, Ancient : 75 ; Legend re Horus 85.

Ekkpahian, sub-tribe of Ibo : and unnatural copulation 34-6.

Ekoi, Semi-Bantu tribe : 65, 79.

Eku, phallic figures : 82 *et seq.*